IDEAS THAT CHANGED THE WORLD

THE EARLY INVENTIONS

ILLUSTRATED BY ROBERT INGPEN
TEXT BY
PHILIP WILKINSON & JACQUELINE DINEEN

CHELSEA HOUSE PUBLISHERS
New York • Philadelphia

First published in the United States in 1995 by
Chelsea House Publishers

First Printing
1 3 5 7 9 8 6 4 2

Simplified text and captions by **Jacqueline Dineen**
based on the *Encyclopedia of Ideas that Changed the
World* by Robert Ingpen & Philip Wilkinson

Editor	Diana Briscoe
Project Editor	Claire Watts
Designer	Design 23
Art Director	John Strange
Design Assistants	Karen Fergusom
	Victoria Furbisher
DTP Manager	Keith Bambury
Editorial Director	Pippa Rubinstein

ISBN 0–7910–2766–X

Printed in Italy

CONTENTS

Introduction...... 8
The First Tools...11

Making Fire...24

Life & Death.....30
Growing Food...36

Plowing the Land......................44

Shelter & Refuge...52
Building to Last...60

Keeping Time...74

Cures & Remedies.......82
Further Reading..........90
Index......................91

Introduction

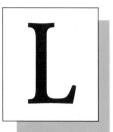ife was hard for the first true humans who lived on Earth. They had no comfortable houses. For food they had to hunt and gather what they could, finding out by trial and error what was good to eat and what was poisonous. If they were ill, there were no medicines – so most people probably died very young. When they died, their bodies would be buried ceremoniously, perhaps with their belongings alongside them. These early graves show us that our ancestors used rituals, one of the activities that sets humans apart from other animals.

The earliest inventions and discoveries were to do with sheer survival. One of the first things people learned was how to make fire. This allowed them to cook food, keep warm, and defend themselves against enemies. The invention of basic tools allowed early people to prepare food and make better shelters. These skills led in turn to advances in farming, giving people more control over their food supply, and in building, bringing them more comfort. Meanwhile, natural curiosity about food plants led people to discover that some types were not only good for you but also helped to cure some illnesses. The first medicines had arrived.

Many people owed their lives to these early inventors and scientists. But it did not stop there. People were unable to resist the urge to take their inventions further, to go on pushing at the limits of human knowledge. Take farming. It was not enough to choose the best crops and cultivate them. Farmers wanted to get better yields, to irrigate (water) their soil, and to find better ways of plowing their fields. The result, achieved by hundreds of years of experiments, was better harvests and more land brought under cultivation.

With more efficient farming came larger supplies of food, which meant that some people could leave the fields and do other jobs, such as making things or taking part in government and administration. Such people, working away from the natural clock of the sun, needed to tell the time. This led to the invention of timekeeping devices like water clocks and sand-glasses. As always with inventions, one thing leads to another.

Architecture was also developed. Brick and stone buildings were made to last and many were decorated with great skill and imagination. So the temples of ancient Egypt and the Middle East became huge religious symbols – buildings had already come a long way from the simple shelters of the first people. Such temples remind us that, from earliest times, inventions have catered to our spirits and our imaginations, as well as our need to survive.

PHILIP WILKINSON

THE FIRST TOOLS

Millions of years ago, our ancestors began to walk on two legs and to use stones as weapons and tools. From that time, human history has been firmly bound up with the discovery and invention of new tools.

W hen the dinosaurs died out sixty-five million years ago, primitive mammals began to take over. Some species did not survive and eventually became extinct. Others evolved into the mammals on the Earth today. One group of mammals developed in quite a different way from the others

△ *Early people found that sharp flints could be used as tools for killing and cutting.*

◁ *Bone and wood as well as stone were used for making early tools.*

to become the early ancestors of humanity. About sixty million years ago, this group of squirrel-like creatures took to the trees. They developed strong limbs to climb and swing in the branches. Their front paws became flexible so that they could grasp fruit and insects. Life in the trees was dangerous because the leaves could hide enemies. The brains of these tree-dwellers began to expand so that they could outthink predators.

Some of these mammals moved down from the trees to live on the ground about fifteen million years ago. Perhaps food in the forests had grown scarce and these

HOW THE FIRST PEOPLE DEVELOPED

2,000,000 years ago
Homo habilis appeared in Africa. He was the first hominid to make tools.

1,500,000 to 500,000 years ago
Homo erectus spread through Africa, Asia and Europe. He was the first hominid to use fire, live in caves and build huts.

400,000 to 50,000 years ago
Homo sapiens lived in Africa, Asia, and Europe.

100,000 to 30,000 years ago
Homo sapiens Neanderthalis, a species of *Homo sapiens*, appeared.

From 50,000 years ago
Homo sapiens sapiens first appeared in Africa, then spread to Europe about 35,000 years ago. This hominid was the direct ancestor of modern people.

creatures had to come down from the trees to feed. By now, they looked more like apes. By four million years ago, these mammals, known as "hominids," had begun to walk on two legs. Their front paws had developed into hands with fingers capable of holding sticks and stones. All the inventions and discoveries that we know and take for granted today stemmed from these simple beginnings.

FINDING TOOLS

The hominids' upright posture was a very important development. Now their hands were free to make and use tools. Like many early discoveries, the use of tools probably began by accident. Perhaps the hominids realized that sticks were useful for digging up roots. Stones could be

used to crush or chop. Before long, someone noticed that some stones had sharp edges which could be used to cut up meat and plants.

At first, the hominids found suitable sticks and stones when they needed them. Someone who wanted to cut up a piece of meat found a sharp-edged stone which happened to be lying around. When the meat was cut, the stone was discarded.

MAKING TOOLS

The next stage required more thought. The early hominids realized that they did not have to look for sharp stones. They could use one stone to chip away at another until it had a sharp edge. Early toolmaking had begun. This was an important moment – for the first time, a group of mammals did not have to rely on their own teeth and claws to kill and cut up food. They could use tools to help them to perform more efficiently.

As far as we know, the first toolmakers lived in East Africa about two million years ago. Flint tools have been found on the shores of Lake Turkana in northern Kenya and in the Olduvai Gorge near Lake Victoria. The hominid species that made these early tools has been named *Homo habilis* which means "handy" or "toolmaking man." *Homo habilis* could stand and walk upright and his brain was nearly half the size of the modern human brain. These hominids were the first true human beings.

The tools of these early people were simple pebbles with flakes chipped away to form a cutting edge. Some tools had long, flat blades. Others had shorter, more pointed ends. Early people did not

▷ *Early people made a variety of tools but the hand ax was the most common type. It had two sharp edges and could be used for cutting, grinding, scraping and pounding.*

Pebble tools
*Small tools made by removing
a few chips from a pebble.*

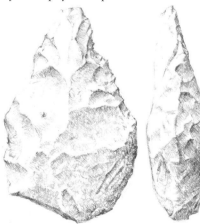

Core tools
*Tools made by removing flakes
from a core of flint.*

Flake tools
*Small cutters and scrapers made
from flakes cut from a flint core.*

Blade tools
*Flakes of flint worked
to make tools for
cutting and boring.*

grow or farm any food, so they had to find food for every meal and most of their time was spent hunting small mammals and grubbing around to find plants. Tools would have been useful for killing and skinning animals, cutting up meat and shredding plants. People also needed shelter and clothing to keep them warm. Sharp tools would help them cut branches to make shelters. Flat-bladed tools would have been useful for scraping animal skins to make simple clothes.

the off-cuts are called "flake tools." Once people realized that they could shape flint in different ways they could make special tools for each job.

HAND AXES

The development from the earliest pebble tools to specialized tools took thousands of years. The first more elaborate tool was an oval hand tool with a double-sided edge. This led to the development of the "hand ax." Hand axes were made

Many types of stone were used to make tools, but flint was the best because it gave a tough, hard edge. People had to search for pieces of flint the right size and shape to make the tools they wanted.

CHOPPERS, CUTTERS AND SCRAPERS

At first, people made general-purpose tools which could be used for chopping, cutting and scraping. The size and shape of the tool depended on the stone it was cut from. Then, people discovered that they could get more than one tool from a single stone.

Many early tools were made from flint, a hard stone which breaks into fragments with sharp edges. To make tools, people chipped flakes off the flint. Some flakes were long and sharp enough to make into separate tools. The shaped piece of flint is known as a "core tool." Tools made from

by chipping away small flakes from a stone, usually with a piece of bone or hard wood. The hand ax was oval or triangular. One end was chipped away to a fine point. The other end was broad enough to be gripped in the hand.

The first hand axes were probably made in Africa between 1.4 and 1.2 million years ago. By this time, a new species of human had replaced *Homo habilis*. This species is known as *Homo erectus*, or "upright man." These people lived between 1.5 million and 500,000 years ago and spread from Africa into Asia and Europe, where examples of hand axes have been found. People living in the Far East do not seem to have discovered hand axes, however. Remains found at a *Homo erectus* site at the Choukoutien cave, near Beijing in China, shows that the people there had only simple chopping tools.

THE RIGHT TOOL FOR THE JOB

Tools could be shaped more precisely with bone or wood than they could by simply banging them with another stone.

Flakes from core tools could be shaped into very sharp, thin knives. People learned to chip the core carefully so that the flakes were the shape they wanted. For example, if the core was shaped into a curved oval, a long strip could be cut from the curved side. The flake would be rounded with thin sharp edges. It could be used as a knife or a scraping tool without any further shaping. This is called the "Levalloisian" method of tool-making, after a site near Paris where

STONE-WORKING TECHNIQUES

Early people used several methods of making stone tools. Some tools were made by simply banging one stone against another. For others, tiny flakes were chipped off to give a very sharp edge. As toolmaking progressed, people learned to use a variety of methods to produce the effect they wanted.

A pebble was used to remove flakes from another stone.

Wooden hammers were sometimes used to get a more precise shape.

To get a razor-sharp edge, tiny flakes were removed using a bone burin with a sharp point.

Levalloisian technique
When the right stone had been found (1), the core was shaped very precisely (2–5). The arrows show the direction of the toolmaker's strokes. Then, the toolmaker aimed a single blow with a stone to remove a finished sharp tool (6).

1

2

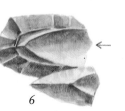

3

4

5

6

examples of these tools were found.

Now people could make different tools to suit their needs. Hand axes were heavier than flake tools and could be used as weapons against enemies as well as for hunting and chopping wood. Light, sharp flake tools were better for cutting, skinning, slicing and shredding.

NEANDERTHAL TOOLS

Neanderthal people appeared about 100,000 years ago. They are named after the Neander Valley in Germany, where their bones were first found. They were a species of *Homo sapiens*, or "wise man," from which modern human beings are descended. Neanderthal people looked

▷ *Hunters combined flint with other materials to make weapons.*

1 Serrated flint knife
2 Ax with a stone head and a shaft made of antler
3 Bone weapon
4 & 5 Bone harpoons attached to shafts with twine
6 Finely carved flint knife

OLDUVAI GORGE

Much of what we know about the first hominids comes from studies made at Olduvai Gorge in northern Tanzania. Millions of years ago, there was a large lake here. Animals living in the area, including the early hominids, came to the lake to drink. Rivers flowing into the lake deposited silt. These silt deposits gradually filled the lake up and rock layers began to form. All this took millions of years to happen. Then a river began to cut its way through the rock, gradually forming what is now the Olduvai Gorge. As the gorge deepened, more and more ancient rock layers were exposed. They contain the fossilized remains of animals that lived in the area in the past.

Studies were made of the fossils but at first no one realized that there were hominid remains among them. Louis (1903–72) and Mary (1913–) Leakey were fossil experts, or "paleontologists," who studied the gorge in the 1930s. They found fragments of fossilized bone which proved to be from early hominids. The Leakeys named their find *Homo habilis*. In 1972, the Leakeys' son, Richard (1944–), found the skull and leg bones of a two million year old *Homo habilis*. Examples of *Homo erectus* were found in higher layers of rock, showing that they were more recent. Many different types of tools were also found in the gorge. Their position in the rock layers helps to date them and show which hominids made them.

2   3   4   5   6

TOOLS FOR BORING

The discovery of metal allowed toolmakers to make stronger tools with a narrower point.

A metal awl with a wooden handle could pierce the toughest materials without breaking (1–3).

A more efficient way of making a hole was to use a bow drill (4). The drill was pushed down hard. As the twine untwisted, the drill turned, forcing the bit into the material.

To be more effective, the tool had to remove some of the material from the hole. The ancient Assyrians and the Romans both used drills with two-edged bits or with spoon bits (5) which did this.

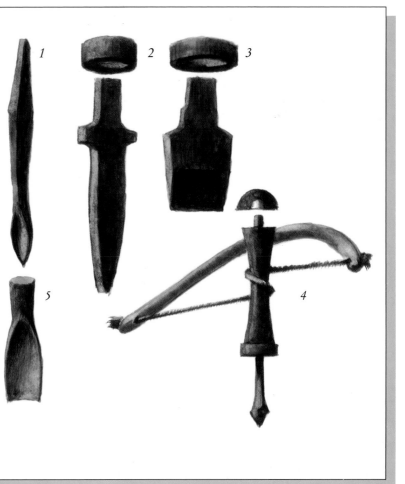

brutish, but they had bigger brains than modern people and were quite intelligent. They spread throughout western Asia and Europe. At this time, the world was in the grip of an Ice Age. Neanderthal people probably wore animal skins to keep warm. Flint scrapers have been found at their sites. These could have been used for scraping fat from skins to make them into clothing.

◁ *Tools and weapons*
1 Antler ax
2 Stone blade in bone haft
3 Serrated stone saw
4 Bone awl
5 Flint arrowheads
6 Bone harpoon head
7 Flint hand ax
8 Bone barbed fish hook
9 Stone adz with
   wooden handle

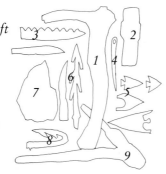

The Neanderthals were the first to make proper use of flake tools. In fact, they cut the flakes they wanted and then threw away the core. They did not just pick up pieces of flint at random, but searched until they found stones suitable for cutting off flakes of exactly the right shape and size for the purpose. From these flakes, they made small spearheads, hand axes and knives. Their knives had one sharp edge and one blunt edge, like modern knives. The Neanderthals also developed a type of saw by cutting notches in the sharp edge of a flint blade.

HUMAN ANCESTORS

A new species of people appeared about 50,000 years ago. These people, called *Homo sapiens sapiens*, are our own direct ancestors. They began to produce a variety of tools and weapons. Some of these were made from bone instead of stone. They also designed a range of implements for making their tools. They used knives, bone or wooden hammers, and a bone tool called a "burin," which was used for cutting tiny flakes to get a very sharp finish.

These implements allowed people to make far more delicate and precisely shaped tools than before. They still made knives and other tools from flint, but they could shape pieces of bone into pins, needles, burins and awls. They could now make clothes by sewing skins together.

Toolmakers also learned how to join a blade or ax head to a wooden shaft. They used this technique, called "hafting," to make arrows, spears, and axes.

THE FIRST FARMERS

By about 12,000 years ago, groups of hunters had spread to most parts of the world. Then, 2,000 years later, there was a major new development in world history. Instead of moving from place to place following herds of animals, people began to settle down and farm the land. These first farmers needed a whole new range of tools for preparing the land and harvesting crops. They made axes for clearing forests, hoes to turn the soil, and sickles for cutting the crops.

The sickle had a long, crescent-shaped blade and a wooden handle. It was one of the most important tools for these early farmers, but it was often difficult to find long pieces of flint to make the blade. The ancient Egyptians came up with a new idea. They made wooden sickles with a row of flint blades along the cutting edge.

The early farmers needed a plentiful supply of flint to make their tools. Until this time, people had relied on searching for suitable flints on the ground. Now,

THE DEVELOPMENT OF THE SICKLE

The first sickles were probably made about 10,000 years ago in Mesopotamia.

The ancient Egyptians used a wooden shaft with a row of flint bl ades to form the cutting edge.

△ *Copper-bladed sickles were not very strong and were difficult to keep sharp. People started working copper about 8,000 years ago.*

Sickles made of bronze (a much harder metal) were used by the Egyptians and Babylonians from about 3400 B.C. onward.

This iron sickle, dating from about 3,000 years ago, is very similar to the shape of those used for harvesting in Europe until well into the nineteenth century.

CLOTHES

Homo sapiens sapiens used their more sophisticated tools to make clothes from animal skins. First, the skins had to be prepared so that they did not crack and fall apart. The skin was stretched out on the ground and scraped clean of fat with a scraper tool. Then, it was smoothed with a bone tool to make it more supple.

When the skin was ready to use, it was cut to shape with stone knives. Holes were punched along the edges with an awl. The edges of the skins were sewn together using a bone needle and a length of sinew.

The skins were used to make tunics or coats, and skirts or trousers.

The edges of the garments were sometimes decorated with shells, and people wore necklaces made from shells or bone.

they began to mine underground. Miners sunk shafts about thirty feet (nine meters) deep into the earth and dug out the best flint with picks made from deer antlers.

METAL TOOLS

Then, about 8,000 years ago, a new and exciting advance was made in western Asia. This was the discovery of metal, and it opened up a whole new range of possibilities.

Copper was the first metal to be used in most early civilizations. It was a soft metal which was easy to shape but not very strong. Early metalworkers discovered that hammering the cold metal made it stronger. Copper mixed with other metals such as nickel or tin was stronger than copper on its own. Bronze was the first "alloy," or mixture of more than one metal. Iron later replaced other metals for many tools and weapons.

Some metal tools were copies of older stone or wooden tools – copper and bronze crescent-shaped sickles began to replace wooden ones. Other metal tools were completely new designs.

WORKING IN WOOD

As civilization progressed, people found that they needed more things to make life comfortable. They wanted to trade, so they needed ships. They built permanent houses instead of rough shelters. They needed a large range of household objects. Many of these things were made from wood. Carpenters were among the most important craft-workers of ancient times and they needed a range of tools.

Many early tools have been lost, but archaeologists have found important evidence at an ancient Assyrian site. For cutting and shaping wood, Assyrian carpenters used metal axes, saws, chisels and the "adz," a tool with an arched blade at a right angle to the handle.

The craft-workers of ancient Greece must have had a variety of tools for the skilled work they did. Paintings on Greek pottery show carpenters, cobblers and metalworkers, together with the tools they used. Sculptors needed tools to shape the magnificent statues and carvings we can still see today. They must have had fairly sophisticated tools to achieve this range of work. It is hard to be sure what these tools were like because little evidence has emerged from Greece itself.

SPREADING IDEAS

Most of our knowledge about tools in the ancient world comes from the Romans. But the Romans adopted many Greek ideas when they conquered the Greek empire, so it is likely that many of their tools are based on Greek ones. Roman carpenters had frame-saws and bow-saws for cutting wood, and two types of drill. The plane was used for the first time in the Roman period. They also had hammers, chisels, axes, adzes and rasps.

By the Middle Ages, tools had progressed still further. Carpenters began to use a vice for holding wood while they worked on it, and a lathe for turning wood while they shaped it. They also used a brace for holding and turning a drill bit, and a T-shaped auger for boring wide holes. Standard tools became more varied. There were different types of saws, hammers, axes, adzes, chisels and rasps for doing different jobs. Many of the tools were similar to those found in the carpenter's workshop today. Hand tools had come a long way since the first crudely carved pebble.

▷ *This medieval carpenter is turning a piece of wood on a lathe driven by a bow. This works on the same principle as the bow drill. Nearly everything was made of wood in medieval times, so the carpenter needed a wide range of tools.*

▽ *By the Middle Ages, carpenters and other craft-workers had many of the hand tools available today.*

1 Auger
2 Brace and bit
3 Froe for splitting wood
4 Clamp
5 Fretsaw
6 Rasp
7 Plane
8 Bow drill
9 Ax

6

7

8

9

MAKING FIRE

By harnessing fire, people began to control one of the forces of nature. Now, they could make night into day, and keep warm even in the coldest temperatures.

A s early hominids began to move out of Africa and spread around the world, they found that some climates were too cold for them to live in. To survive there, they needed to make another important discovery: the use of fire. The first hominid to use fire was probably *Homo erectus* who was more intelligent than earlier species. Archaeologists have discovered evidence of fire at the *Homo erectus* site at Choukoutien in China. Ashes, charred bones and charcoal have been found in a

large cave where people lived 300,000 to 400,000 years ago. The bones, mainly of deer, were probably the remains of meals that had been cooked over the fire.

People had watched fires started by natural causes such as lightning for many thousands of years before they first

△ *Lightning was a natural cause of fire.*

▷ *Turning a stick between the hands was one method of making fire, but the stick had to be pressed hard against a piece of wood at the same time. The bow drill was a more efficient method because it made the stick spin faster and caused more friction between the stick and the hearth.*

thought of making fire for themselves. People were probably terrified of fire at first, just as other animals were. As they got used to seeing fires, they realized that they would come to no harm if they took care. Fires gave off tremendous heat as they raged across the countryside, and they lit up the night sky. People began to see that fire's light and heat could be useful. They discovered that they could light a bundle of twigs in a forest fire and carry the flaming twigs back to the cave or camp where more wood could be set alight to provide warmth and light. If the fire was kept stoked up with fuel, it would burn for as long as they wanted it.

COOKING FOOD

Fire made a great difference to people's lives. For the first time, they could venture into places too cold to live in without it. They could also make their food tastier by cooking. Early hominids ate meat before they discovered fire, so they must have eaten it raw. Raw meat is tough and difficult to chew, but cooking makes it tender. This fact was probably discovered by accident. Someone may have dropped some food into the fire and found to their surprise that it tasted far better afterwards, or perhaps they ate meat from an animal killed in a forest fire.

Early people often ate meat that had been roasted on a stick over the flames. Sometimes, food was cooked more slowly in the embers of the fire. They may also have wrapped meat in a thick layer of clay and leaves to make a sort of oven which could be put in the fire.

Finding food was a hazardous task. On some days, the hunters would catch nothing. On other days, they might kill an animal that provided far too much meat for one meal. Before the discovery of fire, they had to throw away what they could not eat, or leave it lying where they

▽ *The camp fire not only provided warmth and light, but also kept wild animals at bay.*

A curved lens can concentrate the sun's rays on to a small area. The temperature becomes so high that it sets the dry grass alight.

In California, large "fire lenses" have been found which date from between 1.8 million and 10,000 years ago.

had found it. Fire allowed people to smoke meat and fish to store it for times when supplies were scarce.

NIGHT LIGHT

Fire lit up caves and underground passages where daylight never penetrated, so people could begin to live in these dark places. Before the discovery of fire, people could not do anything after darkness had fallen. Now, when the day's hunting was over, they could sit and make tools by firelight. The points of spears and arrows could be charred in the fire to make them stronger. *Homo erectus* was capable of a primitive form of speech by this time, so perhaps people sat around the fire and discussed the day's hunting or where they would go to hunt the next day. Gathering around the fire at the end of the day may have been the start of community living.

A camp or cave fire also gave the people protection. Early people were under constant threat of attack from wild animals. A fire burning through the night kept animals away. They might skulk in the shadows, but they would not come into its light. Fire in a cave drove out wild animals that lived there. Forest fires could also be useful in the search for food. Terrified animals rushed out of the flames towards the hunters who were waiting for them. The fresh undergrowth that grew back after a fire provided more plant food for animals and people.

MAKING FIRE

People had now learned to make use of natural fires, but it was not very convenient to wait for a forest fire every time heat or light were needed. Perhaps people noticed sparks flying when they were chipping flint tools. If a glowing

spark fell on to dry grass, it could set it alight. Once people realized that they could start a fire by producing a spark in this way, they could light a fire whenever they wanted to. Archaeologists have found stones which they think were used to start fires. Lumps of flint which would not have been suitable for making tools had obviously been banged with other stones to start a fire. Striking flints together was fairly efficient, but using a flint to strike a rock containing a yellow vein of iron pyrites was eventually found to produce better sparks.

People may also have noticed that two dry branches brushing together in the wind sometimes caused sparks. Perhaps they decided to imitate this by rubbing sticks together. Then, they began to devise more efficient ways of creating fire. One of these was to press a round stick hard against a flat piece of wood and rotate it quickly between the palms of the hands. The bow drill was later used to turn the stick very fast and produce a flame more quickly.

FIREPLACES AND HEARTHS

Early people moved around, hunting and gathering plant food. They followed the same route each year, stopping at places where they knew the hunting was good. At night, they found a cave or made a shelter where they could sleep. Sometimes they stayed in one camp for a few days before moving on. The earliest fires would simply have been a pile of sticks in the cave or outside the shelter.

When people began to build huts, they made permanent fireplaces. The earliest

◁ *The hunters brought back the animals they had killed that day. The meat was cut up and roasted on the fire. Smaller pieces could be pierced with sticks and held in the flames.*

FIRE AND FOOD

Fire made a difference to the way in which people developed. Early hominids had large, flat molars set in heavy jaws, so that they could chew tough raw meat. Once people began to cook their meat, their teeth and jaws became smaller. Early hominids also had large canine teeth which they used for tearing food, as apes and monkeys do. The canine teeth of *Homo erectus* were smaller.

Ape's skull

Homo erectus's *skull*

Homo sapiens's *skull*

were shallow pits, sometimes surrounded by stones. Later, people built hearths with a large flat stone as the base and raised sides to hold the fire and ashes.

Wood was the main fuel for these fires, and at first people used it for both heating and light. Gradually though, they began to make special lamps which burned oil made from animal fat. Some lamps were made from a large bone with a hollow in it. Others were cut from soft rock such as sandstone. The dish of the lamp was filled with the fat, and a wick made of moss was added. The wick burned until all the fat had been used up.

The discovery of fire made a huge difference to the lives of early people. Not only did they now have warmth and light, but their way of life began to change too, from their diet to the hours they slept and woke.

LIFE & DEATH

As survival became easier for people, they began to consider the world around them. They searched for causes and meanings to problems or events in their lives, such as birth, death, disease and bad harvests.

L ife was hard for the early hominids. The search for food and shelter was so demanding that it left little time for anything else. But at some point, about 80,000 years ago, some of these early people found time to establish rituals and ceremonies. The earliest of these were concerned with burying the dead. Animals do not bury their dead and the earliest people did not either. The first burials must have occurred after people had begun to think about things other than hunting and keeping warm.

THE FIRST GRAVES

We do not know exactly when the first burials happened. Many ancient graves have been discovered but there may be older ones which have yet to be found.

△ *Birth and death were two of the puzzles which led people to develop religious beliefs.*

▷ *People probably decorated their bodies with paint and wore special costumes for early rituals. Music and dancing would have been included. Some early ceremonial sites, such as the huge standing stones of Stonehenge in England, show that people attached great importance to religion, but we can only guess at the exact content of these ceremonies.*

ANIMAL MAGIC

Animals were part of Neanderthal people's beliefs and rituals, probably because they were such an important part of life. A stone box found in a cave in Switzerland was filled with the skulls of cave bears. Bears' limb bones were placed around the walls. Other examples of rituals featuring cave bears have been found in France, Germany and the former Yugoslavia.

One of the earliest settlements in Europe was at Lepenski Vir on the banks of the river Danube. The community dated from about 5000 B.C. Strange heads carved in stone have been found near the center of each house. The faces have staring eyes and thick, down-turned lips and seem to represent a fish god. The people may have worshiped fish gods because the river provided much of their food.

Goats were important sources of meat, milk and skins to early people, and often became important symbols in the first religions. Goats were represented in the early religious festivals of Greece. These ceremonies gradually evolved into theater as we know it. The word "tragedy," which is used to describe some plays, comes from the Greek word "tragoidia" which means "goat-song."

As far as we know, Neanderthal people were the first to bury their dead. They seem to have performed ritual ceremonies which suggest that they had some religious beliefs by this time.

Graves have been found in the earth floors of caves where Neanderthal people lived. The graves are shallow, but even a shallow grave must have taken a long time and a lot of effort to dig with simple stone tools and digging sticks. The body was often placed on its side, with the knees drawn up to the chin, as though the person were asleep. Some bodies were buried with tools, so the Neanderthals may have believed in an afterlife in which people needed their earthly possessions.

A grave found at Teshik-Tash in Uzbekistan contained the skeleton of a small boy. The boy, who had died when he was eight or nine years old, was buried in a shallow grave in a cave high in the mountains. His head was surrounded by pairs of horns from the Siberian ibex, a goat which still lives in this region. Perhaps these animals were an important source of food and skins for the people who lived there. The bones were arranged like a crown around the boy's head, suggesting that his burial involved some sort of ceremony.

GIFTS FOR THE AFTERLIFE

It is difficult for us to piece together information about early burials. The graves that have been discovered show that different groups of people had different ideas and customs. Bodies have been positioned in various ways in the graves. Some people were buried with nothing, others had tools with them. Some bodies were buried with food and cooking vessels, perhaps for their journey to the afterlife.

Music, dance and theater all developed from ancient religious ceremonies. Performances were probably intended to honor or thank the gods, or to keep away evil spirits. Here Native American shamans perform a ritual with poisonous snakes.

These graves do give us some clues about people's lives, however. A mountain cave at Shanidar in Iraq contains the grave of a man who died about 60,000 years ago. The man was about forty when he died, which was a long life in those days. He lived at a time when all men were expected to hunt, yet his arm and shoulder were badly deformed.

He could not have hunted with a useless arm, so his companions must have looked after him and found extra food to feed him. These people seem to have learned to care about others. When this man died, his body was laid on branches and scattered with flowers from the hillsides. Some of these flowers have been known for their healing properties since ancient times. Perhaps the Neanderthals believed the flowers would heal the man in his afterlife.

Archaeologists have found some evidence of ancient musical instruments, so religious ceremonies may have involved music and dancing. People played bone flutes and pipes, rattled bracelets made from small pieces of bone or tusk and beat drums.

The earliest drums were large, flat animal bones which were banged with a bone or an antler. Drums were also made from wood or bone with skin stretched across them.

EARLY GODS

When early people began to think about the world around them, they found it puzzling and frightening. They knew nothing about science and could not explain why the weather changed, why food was sometimes plentiful and sometimes scarce and why strange and disastrous things sometimes happened. The only explanation they could find was that everything was controlled by invisible gods. Early gods were often represented by animals or other symbols. The earliest gods worshiped in Egypt date from before the first nomads settled on the banks of the Nile. They often took the form of animals or birds such as lions, monkeys or crocodiles.

The gods and their mysterious ways became even more crucial when farming developed. Farmers depended on the weather and the environment for their survival, as they do today. If the crops failed, there would be no food. The crops could fail because the rains did not come, or because there was too much rain. Many things could happen between

▽ *In many cultures throughout the world, food was offered to the gods to thank them for providing a good harvest.*

sowing the seeds and reaping the harvest. Early farmers believed that everything depended on pleasing the gods. Their own actions could please the gods or make them angry. If the gods were angry, the crops would not grow. Many early gods represented the weather, the soil and even the crops themselves.

PLEASING THE GODS

The Sumerians farmed the fertile valley between the Tigris and Euphrates rivers, in what is now Iraq between about 4000 and 3000 B.C. By about 3500 B.C., they had built up a sophisticated civilization with large cities. The early Sumerians believed that their only reason for being on the Earth was to please the gods. When they were not praying, they left statues of themselves to pray for them in their absence.

Most of the prayers of these early peoples were concerned with the weather. They prayed to rain gods for rain, and to earth gods for rich soil and successful crops. Many religions had a sun god who was the most important because all life depended on the sun rising each day. After a successful harvest, people gave thanks by making offerings to the gods. Harvest festivals are still held today.

In ancient Greece, festivals of song and dance were performed in honor of the gods. Speaking parts were gradually introduced and then whole plays were written about the gods. People wore costumes and masks to show the characters they were playing. These religious festivals were the earliest form of theater. All modern theater has its roots in these ancient rituals.

△ *Many early religions made statues, or "totems," of their gods.*

GROWING FOOD

Gradually, people discovered that they could produce their own food instead of wandering in search of it. As they settled down together in one place, communities began to develop.

P eople lived by hunting or gathering food for nearly two million years. They discovered which plants were edible and learned to follow herds of migrating animals over long distances. But eventually most groups of people stopped this nomadic way of life and became farmers.

When the early hominids appeared, the world was in the grip of the last Ice Age. Foods such as leaves, fruit, roots, berries and nuts were plentiful in warmer areas but as people spread north into icy regions, they found that they could only gather plants for a short part of the year. For the rest of the time, they had to rely on hunting wild animals such as the mammoth and the reindeer, which could survive in these conditions. These animals also had to find food in a hostile climate and they were constantly on the move.

△ *Goats were among the first animals to be domesticated to provide meat, milk and skins.*

▷ *Early farmers cleared land by hacking down trees and shrubs and burning the undergrowth. "Slash and burn agriculture," as this is known, is still practiced today in some parts of the world.*

HOW WHEAT CHANGED

About 10,000 years ago in eastern Mediterranean lands, early farmers started to collect seeds of wild wheat. They looked for plants with full heads of seeds that were easy to thresh. Modern wheat developed from this selection process over thousands of years.

Naturally growing wild wheat

Wild, but cultivated or collected

Domestic wheat

Then, about 15,000 years ago, the climate began to change. The weather gradually became warmer and the ice began to melt. First, coniferous forests began to spread northward. Then, as the weather became warmer still, forests of deciduous trees such as oaks began to grow and flourish. Ice Age animals died out or moved north, and new animals such as deer, elk and wild pig appeared in the forests. Glaciers melted, leaving lakes where fish and waterfowl could live.

A NEW SOURCE OF FOOD

Life became more comfortable, but it also presented new problems. There was less meat because the animals living in the forests were much smaller and harder to track. People had to look for other sources of food. Some groups discovered that if they lived on the banks of a lake or a river, they could take advantage of the water and the land. They learned to fish and catch waterfowl. They made dug-out canoes and a new range of tools such as harpoons and fish hooks. In other places, hunters studied the movements of forest animals and learned to track them. These animals did not migrate over long distances so there was now no need for people to follow herds. People began to settle in more permanent groups.

At about the same time, people started

Bread has been an important food for people all over the world for thousands of years.

1 Ripe wheat was cut with sickles. The first sickles had flint blades.

3 Stones called "querns" were used to grind the grain into flour. The flour was then used to make bread.

4 The loaves were baked in clay ovens.

1

3

to realize that they could provide their own food. They could sow seeds and harvest a crop. They could domesticate animals so there was always a supply of meat without having to hunt.

2 The grain was separated from the stalks and outer husk, or "chaff," by tossing the wheat in the air. The lighter chaff blew away, leaving the grain behind.

WHERE DID FARMING START?

Farming probably started in several places at a similar time. We know that there were farming communities in eastern Mediterranean lands by about 10,000 B.C. Early forms of wheat and barley grew wild on hillsides. These wild grasses had large seeds which could be ground to make flour. People noticed that

2

4

39

seeds accidentally dropped near their camps began to grow. The soil around the camp had been disturbed and this helped the growth. They began to prepare plots of land by removing other plants and turning the soil over. They sowed seeds from the wild grasses. Soon they had flourishing fields of cereal crops. Crops were cut with a sickle or a bone reaping knife – its blade had flint teeth along it.

farmers became so efficient that they could grow more wheat than they needed to feed themselves and their families. This was an important development. For the first time, some people could turn their attention to other types of work. Craft-workers began to make pottery, tools, baskets and jewelry, and to work in wood. They traded with the farmers, exchanging these goods for food.

Domesticated herds must be protected from wild animals and led to water and grazing every day.

IMPROVING ON NATURE

Early farmers began to improve on the wild grasses. The seeds of wild wheat scatter very easily as soon they are ripe. This is nature's way of spreading the seeds, but it was not ideal for cultivation. In wild grasses, the seeds do not all ripen at the same time, so some of the ears of grain had empty husks by the time the farmers came to harvest them. The farmers reaped only the ears which still contained all the grain, and then sowed only seeds from these grasses. Gradually, wheat with nonscattering seeds evolved.

As farming skills and tools improved,

THE FIRST TOWNS

Groups of farming families built mud-brick houses packed tightly together near their farmland. When the mud bricks eventually crumbled or the houses were destroyed by fire, new houses were built on the ruins of the old ones. A high mound called a "tell" or a "hüyük" gradually developed as people continued to build on top of older buildings. When excavated by archaeologists today, they give fascinating clues about how people lived at different times.

Some of these ancient settlements were large enough to be called towns. The first town was probably Jericho, on the river Jordan, but the largest settlement of this period was Catal Hüyük in southern Turkey. Here, craft-workers produced a range of products which could be traded. Farmers needed pots and baskets for storing food, containers for water and tools for working the land. People needed mats to sleep on and clothes to wear. Ornaments and jewelry made life more attractive. Craft-workers began to work stone, make pots, spin and weave cloth and weave rushes. Some craft-workers started to use a black, volcanic, glassy substance called "obsidian." They polished it to make shiny mirrors or shaped it into hard, sharp tools.

Craft-workers needed raw materials for their work. Towns and villages began to trade with each other for these materials and also for the finished crafts and for some foods. Trade links helped people expand their ideas and control and dominate other communities. The great and powerful civilizations that ruled the ancient world all developed from these early farming communities.

CROPS AND ANIMALS

Farmers grew other crops as well as wheat. It was wise to grow several different crops in case one failed. Barley and millet were grown in China. Lentils were a nutritious food grown in some areas such as Syria. Rice was probably first grown in southeast Asia, reaching India and China by about 4000 BC. In Central and South America, farmers grew maize, beans and avocados.

Farmers kept animals for meat, milk and skins. Sheep and goats were among the first animals to be domesticated, though bones at some sites show that farmers sometimes kept gazelles, deer, wild cattle and wild pigs.

TRADING WITHOUT MONEY

Coins were invented in the seventh century B.C. by the Lydians who lived on the eastern shores of the Mediterranean. Before that time, people had to trade by "bartering," or exchanging their goods for things of a similar value.

At first, trading was local. Towns had markets where farmers and craft-workers could exchange their goods. As civilizations developed, trade links between different parts of the world were established. In Sumer, for example, there were few raw materials for building or crafts. The Sumerians had to import what they needed in exchange for the grain they grew on their fertile farmlands.

The earliest traders soon realized that they needed a system of measuring the value of goods. Shells, heads of cattle, gold dust and obsidian were all used as a measure of value for bartering. The Aztecs of Mexico never had money, and continued to barter until their civilization came to an end. The value of something was measured in cloaks or cocoa beans. For example, an Aztec could buy a dug-out canoe for one cloak or one hundred cocoa beans.

By about 5000 B.C., agriculture was beginning to spread further into Europe and Asia. The idea of farming also spread with the movement of people themselves, as some groups searched for new land to cultivate. By 4000 B.C., groups of farmers had settled in Italy, Sicily, Malta, northern Africa, Denmark and Sweden. In about 3500 B.C., farmers from France crossed to Britain in simple boats.

Not everyone became farmers, though. In North America, for example, there were huge herds of bison which provided enough food and skins for the Plains Indians. They had no need to farm. There are still groups of hunter-gatherers today in some parts of the world.

CHOOSING TO FARM

Farmers had to work hard and probably had less leisure time than nomadic people. Even with hard work, a supply of food was not guaranteed. There was always the worry that crops would fail and people would starve. But this lifestyle had advantages over the old, nomadic one. Farming gave people the chance to settle down in one place. Hunting became more difficult as the population of the world increased and animals avoided places where people were living. Perhaps some animals were in danger of dying out because so many had been hunted. If this was so, it made sense to grow crops and domesticate animals in an organized way.

A more settled farming lifestyle gave people more control over what they did. They could develop in different ways and form larger and more sophisticated communities. Some people became more powerful than others, and social classes began to develop, with a ruler and rich traders dominating the poorer workers. As trade routes opened up, people became less isolated. They learned what

other communities were doing and could adopt new ideas themselves. Perhaps the idea of farming spread in this way.

We cannot be sure how different communities began to farm because there is not enough evidence. What we do know is that organized production of food was one of the most important discoveries of ancient times and formed the basis of civilization. It is how most of the world's food is produced today.

Watering the crops was a problem for farmers in dry areas such as the Middle East. They had to invent ways to lift water from a river and carry it to the fields (irrigation). One was the "shaduf" (above) – a pole with a bucket on one end and a weight on the other. The bucket was lowered into the river and filled with water. The weight on the pole helped to lift the bucket so that it could be emptied into an irrigation ditch.

The man (left) is using a shaduf. The boys (right) are raising water with a treadmill. As they pedal, the paddles go round and scoop up the water.

PLOWING THE LAND

When early farmers thought of drawing a branch across the ground to help them turn the soil for sowing, they were on the way to agriculture on a grand scale.

T he first farmers used very simple tools to prepare the land. Forest often had to be cleared to make a plot of land that could be farmed. The usual method was to burn down the trees. The ash left behind was scattered over the cleared area and the farmer turned the soil with a stick. Sticks were also used to dig holes for planting the seeds. Sometimes, the farmer dug a shallow trench or furrow and sowed a row of seeds. Then, he used a bent stick to cover the seeds with soil.

All this took a long time, so each farmer could only manage to cultivate an area large enough to grow food for himself and his family. As populations grew, this method of farming proved inadequate to feed all the people. Some important developments had to be made before food could be produced on a larger scale. One of these was the invention of the plow. As with many ancient inventions, it is impossible to know who first thought of the idea.

△ *Oxen are used for pulling plows because they are strong and because it is easy to make them move in the right direction.*

Farmers were used to turning the soil and making short furrows with a digging stick.

Perhaps someone realized that dragging a stick over a longer distance would do the job more quickly, and that a bigger stick would be even more efficient. A bough with forked branches made a simple but effective plow, pulled along by two people. Another person would follow along behind, guiding the bough to make sure that it was digging into the soil.

THE IDEA SPREADS

No early plows have survived, but archaeologists have discovered scratch marks made by plows under early settlement mounds. These marks and other evidence such as carvings and wall paintings show us how the plow spread. The simple scratch plow, or "ard," first appeared in southern Mesopotamia, where plow marks dating back to 4500 B.C. have been found. Carvings from Uruk and Babylonia also show farmers using scratch plows. From here, the plow seems to have spread to ancient Egypt. Archaeologists excavating an ancient Egyptian tomb dating back to about 2600 B.C. found a picture of a plowing scene. By the time of the pharaohs of the Middle Kingdom, from about 2130 to 1777 B.C., models and wall paintings of farmers using plows were a common sight in

▽ *Early farmers used a stick with a pointed end to make holes or shallow furrows for sowing seeds. A stone ax might sometimes be needed to break up hard, dry soil.*

tombs. The wooden plow was now an established farming tool in Egypt.

ANIMAL POWER

The earliest scratch plows were pulled by people. These plows were strong enough to turn the light, dry soils of the Middle East but it was hard work for men to pull a plow for long. It was still only possible to cultivate small areas of land with plows pulled in this way.

The domestication of animals developed alongside the cultivation of crops. At first, farmers only thought about meat, milk and skins. Then, they realized that larger animals could be used to do work that was too heavy or difficult for men. One of these tasks was pulling the plow.

Oxen were the first domesticated animals to be used for this purpose. A pair of oxen could pull a plow all day long without getting tired. For the first time, farmers could cultivate large fields and grow enough food to feed a nonfarming population as well as themselves.

The use of oxen seems to have been another Mesopotamian development which spread to ancient Egypt. Egyptian tomb paintings and models show oxen drawing plows. These pictures are our best evidence about what early plows looked like. They had a single pole with a pointed end which dug into the ground. This pointed part is known as the "share." The plow was steered by a wooden handle fixed to the share. A beam of wood was tied to the top end of the share. Oxen were harnessed to the beam to draw the plow.

PLOWS IN EUROPE

Wooden scratch plows were suitable for the light soils of Mesopotamia and Egypt, where the weather was dry, but they were

The first plow was probably a branched bough which was dragged along the ground by two men. A third followed, guiding the bough along the furrow.

not so effective on soil that was heavy or wet. Cattle bones found in the lower Danube area of eastern Europe suggest that oxen may have been used to draw plows there as long ago as 4500 B.C.

There is also evidence that plows were being used in Poland and in southern England by about 3500 B.C. It would have been hard work to use a wooden plow on the soils of these rainy northern lands, even if it was pulled by animals. Yet that is the only sort of plow there was in the western part of Earth in these early days of farming. The development that was to turn the plow into an efficient tool for large-scale farming on any type of soil came from another region entirely.

CHINESE SECRETS

In China, a civilization was developing quite independently from the other

△ Oxen were harnessed to the plow by ropes and a wooden beam. They could pull the plow through heavier soils than men could.

civilizations of the ancient world. Trade and conquest in the West had meant the sharing of knowledge and discoveries throughout Western countries. But the Chinese guarded their secrets closely and the Orient was to remain a mystery to the West for thousands of years. Yet it was here that some of the most important developments in all sorts of crafts were made. It was Chinese farmers who discovered that stone could be used to make plowshares much stronger than wooden ones. Stone plowshares dating back to 3000 B.C. have been found in China, and they may have been used for far longer. Farmers also used wooden plows, but stone, though heavy, could cut deeper furrows through difficult soil.

An even more important Chinese discovery was the iron plowshare. Iron was strong and heavy and it could be shaped into a share that would break up soil very effectively. An iron plow was quicker to use than a wooden or stone one, and it could plow heavy soils more easily. Farmers were using iron plows in China by the sixth century B.C., at least 500 years before they were discovered by farmers in the West. The Chinese had two types of metal plow. One was made entirely of iron, which would have been effective but heavy. The other type had a wooden share with iron laid over it.

OVERCOMING THE PROBLEMS

In ancient times, iron was usually heated and then beaten into shape to make "wrought iron." To make it stronger, iron can be melted in a furnace, poured into a mold and allowed to harden. In this hardened form, it is known as "cast iron." Cast iron is a strong, heavy material which could be ideal for making plowshares. However, it is brittle, so a

THE FIRST PLOWS

Though simple, these plows enabled the Egyptians and the Mesopotamians to produce large amounts of food to feed their growing populations.

Handle

Sole

Roman plow or ard, first century A.D.

PULLING THE PLOW

In some parts of the world, farmers still use oxen to pull plows over small plots of land. However, this is not such a satisfactory solution for bigger farms because the animals are slow. During the nineteenth century, farmers began to look at other ways of pulling farm machinery.

Steam engines such as the steam tractor were sometimes used for pulling plows. However, steam-driven machines were cumbersome and it was difficult to direct the plow over the field properly. The tractors were also heavy and flattened the soil, making it more difficult for the plow to turn

it over. Animals only tread down a small amount of earth and do not affect the work of the plow. A steam plow introduced in 1830 used a system of pulleys and cables to connect a plow to a stationary steam engine. However, many farmers preferred to keep to the traditional methods, and horse-drawn plows were still being used in the early part of the twentieth century.

Modern tractors have big wheels which compact the earth to some extent but they are easy to steer and have the power to pull the large, modern plows.

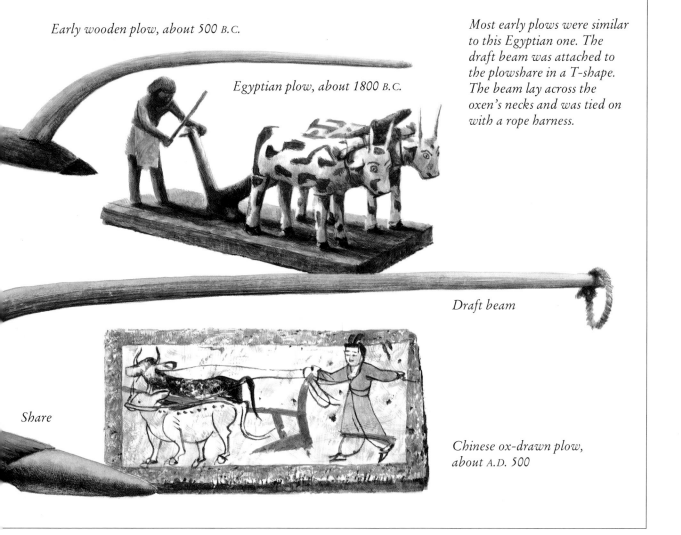

Early wooden plow, about 500 B.C.

Egyptian plow, about 1800 B.C.

Most early plows were similar to this Egyptian one. The draft beam was attached to the plowshare in a T-shape. The beam lay across the oxen's necks and was tied on with a rope harness.

Draft beam

Share

Chinese ox-drawn plow, about A.D. 500

cast-iron plowshare would shatter into fragments if it hit a rock in the soil.

Metalworkers in Europe could not make cast iron at all until the Middle Ages. Intense heat is needed to melt iron and no one in Europe had found a way of making a powerful enough furnace. Yet the Chinese not only managed to produce cast iron, but they also developed better casting techniques so that they could make cast iron which did not break. This was an amazing achievement.

Firstly, the Chinese found out how to make blast furnaces for melting the iron. By the fourth century B.C., they were making furnaces from clay bricks. The clay they used held the heat well, so the

furnaces could reach a high temperature. The Chinese also managed to lower the melting point of iron by mixing it with other minerals. They solved the problem of cast iron's brittleness by keeping the iron at a high temperature for several days, a process known as "annealing."

BIGGER AND BETTER

Once the Chinese had worked out how to make stronger iron, they could design bigger and better plowshares. One problem with early plows was that the earth tended to fall back into the furrow as soon as the plow had passed. By the third century B.C., Chinese farmers had designed a sharply pointed plow with wings that flung the earth away to either side of the furrow. These plowshares could dig deeper furrows than before.

A vertical bar called a "stock" ran from the plowshare to a handle. The plowman moved the handle to control the direction of the share in the soil.

Moldboard

NEAT RIDGES

An even better development for getting rid of the soil from the furrow was the "moldboard." This curved plate above the plowshare turns the soil over and makes it fall in a neat ridge on one side of the furrow. Chinese farmers were using moldboards by the first century B.C.

Moldboards did not appear in Europe until medieval times and even then they were not as effective as the Chinese version. The curved moldboard had a scooping effect which threw the earth well clear of the furrow. European moldboards were flat and pushed the earth away from the plow but not far. The plowman had to keep stopping to clear away soil that had fallen back or stuck to his plow.

Thomas Jefferson, who helped improve agricultural methods in the U.S.

The Chinese also developed another improvement. Soil does not stay the same all the time. It becomes heavy and sticky when it is wet, and light and crumbly when it is dry. There might also be several different soil types within a fairly small area of land. A farmer had to take these differences into consideration when he plowed the soil. He had to lean more heavily on the plow handle to push the point of the plowshare into heavy soil. He had to do the same if he wanted to dig a deeper furrow. The Chinese made a plow that could be adjusted to plow to different depths without the farmer using any extra effort.

EAST MEETS WEST

The Western world did not really know what was going on in China until Europe began to trade with the Chinese. The British and Dutch East India Companies were founded in the early seventeenth century to trade in spices, silks and other products from the East. By the late seventeenth century, the Dutch East India Company had trade routes to China. It was probably these Dutch traders who

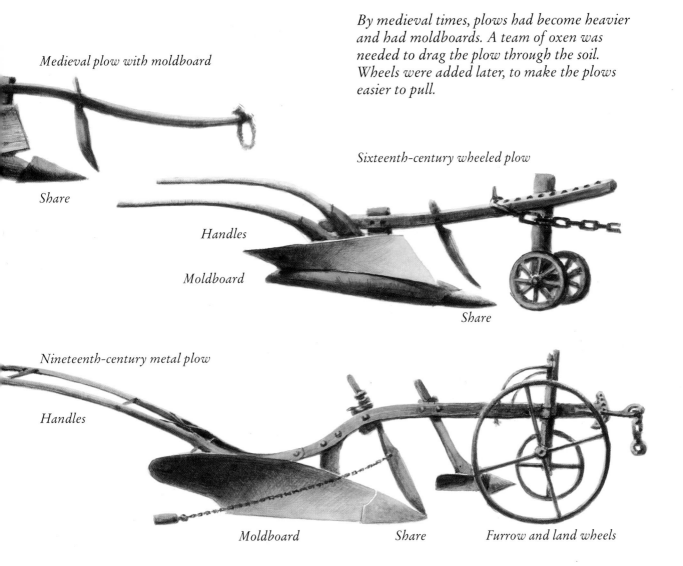

Medieval plow with moldboard

By medieval times, plows had become heavier and had moldboards. A team of oxen was needed to drag the plow through the soil. Wheels were added later, to make the plows easier to pull.

Share

Sixteenth-century wheeled plow

Handles

Moldboard

Share

Nineteenth-century metal plow

Handles

Moldboard   *Share*   *Furrow and land wheels*

brought information about Chinese plows to Europe. The Dutch began to use curved moldboards which they adapted to their own type of soil.

CHANGING THE LANDSCAPE

Farmers in England still used the medieval system of open fields divided into strips. This system was not efficient enough to feed the growing population and, during the eighteenth century, an agricultural revolution swept through the country.

Strip farming was replaced by larger fields surrounded by hedges. The improved plow design was soon adopted

by English farmers who needed to plow these larger fields quickly and efficiently. The new style of plow also spread across other parts of northern Europe and to America. Thomas Jefferson (1743–1826), who became President of the United States in 1801, took a great interest in improving methods of agriculture. Some of his ideas came from France, where he had lived in the years leading up to the French Revolution.

Today's tractor-drawn plow, turning neat furrows in huge modern fields, is a sophisticated machine, but it is still doing the same basic job as the early farmer dragging a stick through the soil.

SHELTER & REFUGE

*The first people relied on caves or trees to keep
them warm and to protect them from wild
animals as they slept, but gradually people
learned to construct shelters from materials that
they found around them.*

A s early people began to
move north, they found
that at night they needed
a place where they could
keep warm and be safe
from wild animals while
they slept. A cave could form a strong
natural refuge, and early people certainly
did use caves for shelter, as the remains of
bones, tools and early graves in hilly
regions of France, Spain and Germany
show. But people spread to many parts of
the world where there are no caves and
must have needed to find other ways of
sheltering.

BUILDING WITH WOOD

Early people must also have been able to
build simple shelters. These temporary
shelters would have been built from
materials that people found around them.
Perhaps the early hunters simply broke
branches off trees and leaned them against
a rock to form a low shelter they could
crawl into to sleep.

△ *A cave provided natural shelter and also
protected the fire from the weather.*

▷ *Huts or tents grouped together in a circle
gave added protection from animals and from
the weather.*

EARLY ARCHITECTURE

Early houses came in a variety of shapes and sizes. At Khiroktia in Cyprus, people built round, domed houses like beehives. Houses in Mesopotamia were usually rectangular and built around a courtyard, but there were also "tholoi," or circular houses. These strange buildings had a rectangular roofed section with a circular, domed room at one end. At Catal Hüyük, there were no streets between the houses. People got about by crossing the rooftops. The doors into the houses were in the roof. Each house had one room set aside as a shrine, a storeroom and a living room with built-in benches and platforms for sleeping, sitting and working on.

Many towns were built with houses crammed together and narrow, winding streets. The towns were often surrounded by a wall to keep out invaders. Jericho, the world's oldest town, was enclosed by a stone wall ten feet (three meters) thick.

Mohenjo-Daro and Harappa in Pakistan were two of the first cities to be laid out on a grid system. The main streets ran in straight lines from north to south. Smaller lanes crossed them from east to west.

Although these shelters disappeared long ago, there are some clues to help piece together a picture of early shelters. The site of a settlement dating back at least 125,000 years has been found at Terra Amata in southern France. Archaeologists have identified holes in the ground where poles were stuck into the soil to make the framework of huts, and the outlines of stones which must have been used to weigh the poles down. Studies of huts made by modern hunter-gatherers such as the Bushmen in Africa help archaeologists to work out what these ancient huts were like.

BUILDING WITHOUT WOOD

It was not so easy to make shelters in the icy wastes of the northern lands, where building material was scarce. As hunters followed mammoths on to the vast, open steppes in Russia and Siberia, they found a bleak landscape whipped by icy winds, where hardly any trees grew. The answer was to build huts from the remains of the mammoths they had killed. The circular wall of the hut was made from stones and large bones, packed with mud. The roof was made of small branches or smaller bones and reindeer antlers.

Shelters could also be made by weaving branches together to form two screens and then leaning them against each other. A screen of branches curved round in a cone became a hut. A framework of long sticks stuck into the ground or weighed down with stones would hold the hut upright. The sticks could be tied together with creepers or grasses, leaving a small gap for a door. Then, more branches could be woven in, or the hut could be covered with grass, leaves, or skins.

Shelters were made from whatever material was easily available. The early farmers of the Middle East built mud-brick houses (1). Wattle and daub huts (2) were common, made by plastering woven branches with mud. Where there was a danger of flooding, people built houses on stilts (3). Nomads made tents from skins (4 & 5). In the north, mammoth bones were used to build strong huts (6).

SHELTER AROUND THE WORLD

People have always adapted their houses to the climate they live in and the materials around them. Around the world, many of these traditional methods of building still survive today.

The Inuit are hunters who live in the frozen Arctic regions of North America and Greenland. In the winter, when it is very cold and there is hardly any sunlight, the traditional Inuit shelter was the igloo, built from large blocks of ice. In summer, they lived in shelters roofed in turf.

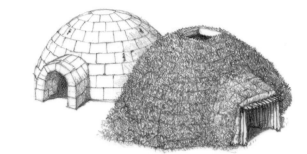

The nomadic peoples of North America followed the migrations of herds of bison across the plains. They used wooden poles and animal skins to make tents. Some made cone-shaped tents, known as tepees. They could be laced up to keep out the bitter winter cold. Others made round huts covered with skins.

In the Middle East, the weather is much the same all the year round. The days are hot and the nights are cold. Early farmers built houses of mud bricks with flat roofs. The roof was supported by wooden rafters. In some places, houses like these are still common.

In the tropics, it is hot and humid all year round. There is heavy rain nearly every day and rivers and lakes sometimes flood. Early people in these regions fished and farmed. They built houses on stilts to keep the floor above flood level. The frame was wood and the walls and roof were thatched.

Tents made from animal hides on a wooden or bone framework probably provided many early shelters. Archaeologists have discovered evidence in Germany which shows how reindeer-hunters made their tents about 15,000 years ago. By this time, the ice was beginning to melt, leaving tundra where reindeer grazed. Reindeer moved faster than mammoths, and hunters had to kill more animals to provide enough meat. The hunters moved on every few days, following the herds north in the spring and south in the autumn.

PORTABLE HOMES

The hunters could never be sure of finding shelter on the bleak tundra, so they devised the tent, a home that was light enough to carry around and quick and easy to set up at the new camp. These tents had a simple cone-shaped framework of poles tied together at the top. The frame was covered with a layer of reindeer skins. If the ground was too hard to dig the poles into the soil, the hunters could weigh the framework down with stones. Some hunters secured the tents with ropes. Ropes made from animal sinew or other flexible material were stretched out from the top of the tent and tied round stones on the ground. In winter, the hunters built a wall of stones or sand around the base to give the tent extra protection against the icy wind. They also built a small fire inside the tent to keep themselves warm.

THE END OF THE ICE AGE

As the climate continued to change and people no longer had to migrate, the need for portable tents was not so great. The weather was warmer and the new forests provided plenty of material for making shelters quickly and easily. It was not

△ *Branches were lashed together with creepers.*

necessary to drag poles and skins around, as hunters could cut wood and make shelters wherever they happened to stop. Making tents from skins had meant that hunters had to kill large animals, and there were fewer such animals about at this time.

There were disadvantages in making temporary shelters each time they settled in a new place. The frame had to be made from long, straight poles which could be difficult to find. It was hard work chopping the wood and trimming off branches with a primitive stone ax. The shelters would probably have been very small and low, and not very comfortable to sleep in. Building a low wall to support the poles or building the hut over a shallow pit gave a bit more height, but the shelters were still not ideal. The biggest disadvantage was that these lightweight shelters did not give much protection against predators.

SETTLERS

By 6000 B.C., people who still lived by hunting and gathering tended to stay in one place for long periods, catching fish or hunting deer. They would chop down trees to make a clearing in the forest and build huts that were bigger and stronger than earlier shelters.

A settlement at Lepenski Vir on the river Danube in Serbia had wooden huts which were shaped like ridge tents. Long, strong poles were leaned against each other in an upside-down V-shape, probably with a fork at the top to hold the long ridge pole. The roofs would have been thatched.

People living in China also built fairly substantial wooden houses from about 5000 B.C. Houses at Pan P'o Ts'un had thatched roofs made of reeds and straw. The roof was supported on wooden poles inside the house. The houses were often round with walls of "wattle and daub," which is made by weaving branches together and plastering them with clay to

△ *Reeds made a useful thatching material.*

give a solid surface. The Chinese also made rectangular houses with a thatched roof that sloped right down to the ground. A pit was dug in the floor to give headroom inside the house.

MUD-BRICK HOUSES

When people settled down in communities, they began to build more permanent houses. Houses were still made of wood in places where there were plenty of trees. But trees were scarce in the areas where farming began, so early farmers had to find another way of making shelters.

People living in Mesopotamia, India and lands around the eastern Mediterranean learned to make their houses from mud bricks or "adobe." They noticed that mud is soft and sticky when it is wet but that it bakes hard in the hot sun. If the mud could be molded into a suitable shape, they could use it to build a wall. To build a wall, the dried mud bricks were laid one on top of the other and stuck together with mortar made from mud. When the building was finished, the outside was plastered with more mud to give extra protection from the weather.

CHANGING SHAPE

Many early houses were round like tents but gradually people began to build rectangular houses. This was more suitable for fitting the buildings together in a settlement. There was not much rain in these regions so the roofs were flat. They were sometimes thatched with reeds. These early brick houses lasted for a long time, and there are still many mud-brick buildings in the Middle East, some of which are thousands of years old. The modern system of making bricks is really only a more sophisticated version of baking clay until it is hard.

MUD BRICKS

At first, mud bricks were shaped by hand but this was laborious and it was not possible to make regular shapes. So the early builders began to press mud into rectangular wooden molds, ramming it down hard into the corners to get a sharp edge. The bricks were left to dry in the sun or baked in an oven. The first bricks were not very successful because the mud cracked as it dried but this problem was solved by adding straw.

BUILDING TO LAST

Once they had mastered the art of working in stone, builders could build magnificent temples, palaces and tombs, designed to last for eternity.

T oday, travelers visiting different corners of the globe see magnificent evidence of past lives, from the pyramids of ancient Egypt on the banks of the Nile, to the ornately carved temples of ancient Greece and Rome, and the lofty medieval cathedrals with spires soaring into the sky. These buildings, some of them thousands of years old, all have one thing in common. They are built of stone.

People had recognized the usefulness of stone from the earliest times. But making small tools from pieces of flint is a very different matter from building a stone house, let alone a huge building. The small pieces of stone that people found on the ground were no good for building. A stone structure has to be made from large

△ *Stone could be quarried by cutting round the edges and then driving wooden wedges into the rock face so that it came away in blocks.*

▷ *Stones sometimes had to be dragged for long distances from the quarry to the site. Some of the stones used to build Stonehenge, in Wiltshire, England, were dragged from the mountains of Wales, over 125 miles (200 kilometers) away.*

blocks cut to a suitable shape for fitting together. This meant quarrying stone from a rock face, taking the blocks to the building site and then cutting them to shape. Attempting these tasks with simple tools must have seemed almost impossible.

MALTA'S MYSTERIOUS TEMPLES

Early civilizations left very little evidence to show how they tackled the problems of using stone. In some cases, archaeologists have been able to work out what must have happened by studying the remains of buildings. In other cases, there is so little to go on that they cannot even do this.

In about 3600 BC, people living on Malta built amazing stone temples at Tarxien, Hal Saflieni and other places on the island. These temples are not like any other buildings of the ancient world. They have separate rooms linked by passages. Each room is divided into a pair of semicircular chambers. The walls of these strange temples are made from massive stones, or "megaliths." Some of the temple walls are twenty-five feet (eight meters) high.

The people who built these extraordinary temples disappeared without a trace and left no evidence of how they worked. But, however they managed it, their achievement was remarkable.

PYRAMIDS ALONG THE NILE

Stone was not used extensively at the time the Maltese temples were built. It was to be another thousand years before a much more famous civilization began to build in stone. The pyramids were built between 2700 and 1700 B.C. as tombs for the pharaohs of ancient Egypt. They tell us a great deal about how the early stone-workers managed with simple tools. Although the Egyptians did not leave much written evidence about their methods, archaeologists have worked out how they could have been built.

The easiest way to transport large quantities of stone was along the river, which may be one reason why the pyramids stand near the banks of the Nile. The outer wall of the pyramid was made from limestone, which was quarried at Tura, on the eastern bank of the river. Limestone is a soft rock which is easy to cut. The Egyptians had copper chisels and sharp saws to remove the stone in large blocks.

The inner core of the pyramid was granite which probably came from Aswan in the south of Egypt. Granite is a very hard rock which would have blunted the Egyptians' copper tools when they tried to cut it. Archaeologists are not certain what method was used, but the Egyptians did somehow manage to cut the large blocks they needed.

These massive blocks of stone, weighing between two and fifty tons, were loaded on to boats. The blocks then had to be taken from the boat to the site of the pyramid. First, a stone causeway was built from the river to the site. The blocks were loaded on to sleighs and dragged up the causeway. The next problem was lifting the blocks to the necessary height. The stones were probably hauled up ramps of stone or packed mud which were specially built for the purpose. The ramps would have to be extended as the pyramid grew taller. These ramps were dismantled when the pyramid was complete.

BUILDING IN THE AMERICAS
The building of the pyramids was the first time a civilization had undertaken such a massive project, with careful planning and a huge work force. But other civilizations also built impressive temples, palaces and tombs using simple tools. The great civilizations of Central and South America, the Maya, the Aztecs and the Incas, ruled their empires at a much later

date than the Egyptians but their way of life was no more sophisticated. Many of their buildings were destroyed by the Spanish conquistadores who invaded Central and South America in the sixteenth century.

▷ *It has been estimated that it took 50,000 people twenty years to build the Great Pyramid at Giza.*

The Maya people lived in the Yucatán peninsula of Mexico between A.D. 300 and 900. Their temples were pyramids or smaller rectangular buildings covered with elaborate carvings. In Egyptian pyramids, the stones were held in place by their own great weight. The Maya learned to use mortar to hold the stones of their buildings together. They were the earliest American civilization to do this. They also built columns and pillars, and designed a type of arch.

The Aztecs, who ruled over a huge empire in Mexico between 1350 and 1521, built their magnificent city of Tenochtitlán on an island in a lake. Nothing remains of Tenochtitlán today, and Mexico City now stands on the site. But at the height of the Aztecs' power, about 200,000 people lived there, making it one of the largest cities in the world. The houses of farmers and craft-workers were made of wattle and daub or mud bricks, but the nobility had fine villas built of stone. Aztec temples were solid pyramids covered with mud bricks or stone. The great temple in the center of Tenochtitlán was 500 feet (150 meters) high. The walls were decorated with sculptures and paintings and two steep flights of steps led up the outside to the top of the pyramid.

THE LOST CITY

The Incas had a great empire in Peru at about the same time as the Aztecs ruled in Mexico. They built fine cities such as Cuzco and Vilcabamba, but one of the most intriguing is the "lost city" of Machu Picchu. For centuries, no one knew about Machu Picchu because there was no mention of it in the histories of the Spanish invaders. But legends about a mysterious Incan city in the mountains led to a search, and the ruins of Machu Picchu were discovered in 1911, on a mountain ridge high in the Andes. Houses, palaces and temples in the city are all built from granite which was cut so precisely that the stones fitted together without mortar. This must have been done with stone hammers and perhaps chisels made of bronze, similar to the tools used by the Egyptians 3,000 years earlier. The buildings are at different levels on the steep mountainside, linked by more than a hundred stairways, some with 150 steps.

Some of the most amazing buildings built in the past are still standing today.

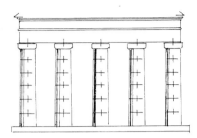

The Parthenon (top) which stands on the Acropolis in Athens, Greece, is a typical example of a Greek temple. Massive lintels are held up by rows of carved pillars. The roof would originally have been tiled. The stones of the columns were held together with iron rods or wooden pegs.

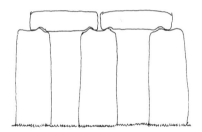

The stone circle known as Stonehenge (center) was built between 2500 and 1500 B.C. The horizontal lintels are fixed to the standing stones with "mortise and tenon" joints. Projecting tenons on the uprights fit into holes called mortises in the lintels.

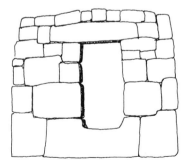

The city of Machu Picchu (bottom) gives us valuable evidence about Inca building styles. The Incas cut their stones so accurately that they fitted together without mortar.

THE TEMPLES OF GREECE AND ROME

Meanwhile, in Europe, buildings were becoming much more sophisticated. At the height of ancient Greek civilization, between 500 and 400 B.C., the Greeks were using blocks of marble or limestone for their temples and public buildings. Some stones were cut so accurately that they fitted together perfectly, but the Greeks also used iron or bronze clamps to hold stones together. Columns were made by standing shaped pieces of stone on top of each other. The stones were lifted into position with pulleys and fixed together with iron rods or wooden pegs.

The Romans were skilled engineers and they had various methods of building. The simplest was to fix regular blocks of stone together with mortar or clamps. But one of their most important contributions to architecture was the use of concrete. Many Roman buildings had concrete walls covered with stone or bricks. One advantage of this method was that

◁ *The great buildings of Egypt, Greece and Rome were often decorated with carvings, sculptures and paintings. Stone was a good material for carving and artists could create religious or heroic scenes, or simply portray everyday life in their work.*

concrete walls could be built by unskilled labor, leaving the stonemasons free to carry out the more skilled and decorative work.

△ *The Greeks developed three styles of column decoration. The Doric style (left) had a plain, square slab at the top. The Ionic style (center) was more slender, with a scroll design on the top, or "capital." In the Corinthian style (right), the capitals were larger and more decorative.*

BUILDING IN CURVES

Until Roman times, most buildings had straight walls supporting a flat or sloping roof. The roof could be supported by the walls themselves, as in the Mediterranean mud-brick houses. It could also be supported by a wooden framework of vertical and horizontal poles, as in wattle and daub structures, or by stone columns as in Greek architecture. Whichever method was used, shapes within the building were basically flat and rectangular.

BUILDING IN CONCRETE

A concrete wall was built by making a wooden mold, called a "form," and pouring concrete into it. When the concrete had set hard, the form was removed.

The great advantage of concrete was its strength. The Romans made their concrete by mixing small pieces of stone with a mortar of lime and sand. The mixture was easy to work, which allowed the Romans to experiment with new shapes in building, such as arches, vaults and domes.

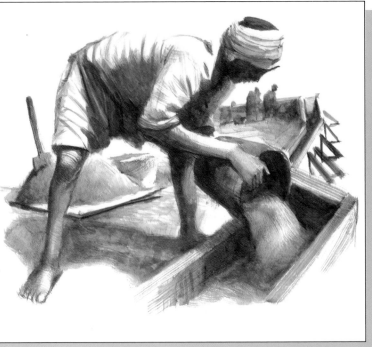

People had made simple domed roofs long before the Romans, using a method called "corbeling." When the builder reached the top of the wall, he laid a row of bricks or stones that jutted slightly into the inside of the building. The next row of stones overlapped a bit more and so on until the stones met in the middle to form a roof. In a rectangular building, the roof was a simple vault. In a square building, the roof was a simple dome.

The Mycenaeans, who lived in Greece around 1300 B.C., built underground domed tombs which can still be seen today. The most famous of these tombs is known as the Treasury of Atreus. It has a corbeled dome made from thirty-four rows or "courses" of stone. The stones were carefully cut so that they formed a curved ceiling surface when they were fitted together.

THE ARCH

The Mycenaean system of corbeling could only be used for fairly small structures. It was the Romans who came up with a scheme for using domes and vaults on a larger scale. The design of many Roman buildings followed the Greek ideas, but the Romans were also influenced by the Etruscans who ruled over central Italy from 800 to 200 B.C. One idea which they adopted from Etruscan building was the arch. The arch is very strong shape, good for supporting a heavy roof.

The walls of the circular Colosseum in Rome are made up of a line of arches. These were built around semicircular wooden frames. The top

◁ *The Treasury of Atreus.*

▷ *The coffered ceiling of the Pantheon in Rome gives the dome a light and airy appearance. The dome is supported by buttresses.*

stone, or "keystone," was put in last. The arch also allowed the Romans to build strong bridges such as the Pons Fabricius in Rome.

By combining the arch with their use of concrete, the Romans began to make vaulted roofs. The simplest style was the "barrel vault." This fitted over a rectangular building with an arch at either end. When the walls and arches had been built, a wooden mold in the shape of the vault was fitted on top of them. Concrete was poured into the mold and left to set. Then the wooden framework was removed. The barrel vault was not just used on rectangular buildings. It could be adapted to suit buildings of different shapes. For example, a square building could be roofed with an intersecting vault made up of two barrel vaults in the shape of a cross.

SUPPORTING A DOME

The Romans also used concrete to help them build domes. One of their most famous domed buildings is the Pantheon in Rome. This circular temple is roofed with a massive concrete dome over 130 feet (forty meters) in diameter. One problem that the builders had to overcome was how to support such a big and heavy dome. They solved this by building the temple walls of solid concrete with an outer shell, or "facing," of brick.

1 Barrel vault
The simplest type of vault is the barrel vault. It is shaped like half a cylinder. Building the vault is like building arches one after another along the length of the building. A barrel vault is suitable for roofing a long, rectangular building with an arch at each end. It is not so good for wide buildings, however, because the height of the vault has to be increased with the width. The Romans covered their barrel vaults with concrete to give a smooth finish.

2 Intersecting vault
This is made by building two barrel vaults at right angles to each other so that they form a cross. The points where the vaults join is shaped like an X. The intersecting vault is useful for roofing square buildings or parts of buildings.

3 Gothic ribbed vault
Barrel vaults were heavy and needed thick walls to support them. A strong wooden frame also had to be made to support the vault while it was being built. Gothic stonemasons designed the ribbed vault in which strong stone "ribs" take some of the strain. Gothic stonemasons also used pointed arches instead of round ones which helped to add height to the vault without increasing the width of the arch.

More ribs
Gothic masons realized that they could use more ribs to provide an even stronger support and to give a more ornamental appearance at the same time. The intricately patterned ceilings of medieval churches and cathedrals are some of the most beautiful in the world.

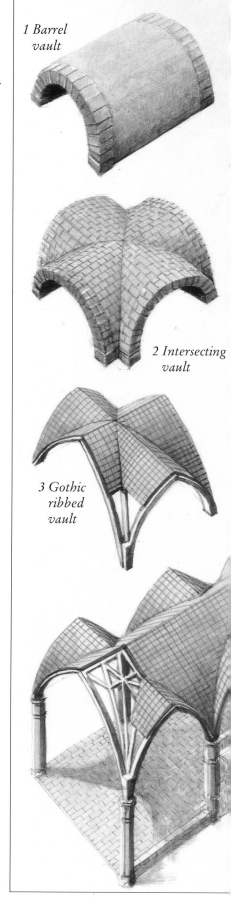

1 Barrel vault

2 Intersecting vault

3 Gothic ribbed vault

GOTHIC ARCHITECTURE

Gothic architecture flourished in Europe between the twelfth and fifteenth centuries, mainly in the building of churches and cathedrals. Its main features are ribbed ceilings, pointed arches and flying buttresses.

The elegant flying buttresses (4) joined the wall at the top of their arches, helping to spread the weight of the vaulted roof over a wider area.

A wooden framework (5) was built over the vaulted stone ceiling to support the outer roof.

△ *A large number of people were needed to work on a building such as a cathedral. Temporary wooden workshops were built on the site for working on individual items and storing equipment.*

To help take the strain of the roof, they added "buttresses," or supports, built against the walls to bear some of the weight. The dome on the Pantheon was made lighter by "coffering" the ceiling. The dome is supported by thick concrete ribs arranged in a pattern of squares. The concrete in the center of the squares is thinner than on the ribs.

The Romans used the Pantheon as a model for many circular buildings with domes. But they did not achieve the next step, which was to build a dome on a square building. The first people to

manage this were the Byzantines, a new civilization which rose up as the Roman Empire declined. Byzantium was the first Christian empire and the Byzantines built magnificent domed churches such as Hagia Sophia in the capital city of Constantinople, now known as Istanbul in present-day Turkey.

BUILDINGS MADE OF LIGHT

The Middle Ages was the period of Gothic architecture in Europe. The main feature of Gothic architecture is the pointed arch. This was more elegant than the earlier,

BYZANTINE DOMES

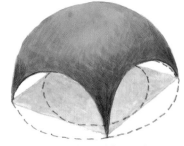

The Byzantines were the first to overcome the problem of building a dome on a square building. The problem is that a square can only support a circle in the four places where it touches.

The outer dotted lines show the diameter of a sphere fitted over the square. Arches would need to be cut in the sphere so that it did not overlap the square. The wall would then be built up to the top of arches. This would give a very shallow dome.

The Byzantine answer was to split the design in two. Arches were formed by curved wedges of stonework on each corner of the building. These were supported on massive stone pillars or piers.

The curved stonework met to leave an open circle that the dome could rest on. The dome could be much higher and the piers and arches would help to spread the weight.

A series of small arches can be built around the square to form an octagon on which to built the dome. These are called "squinch arches."

Corbeling can also be used to fill in the gaps in the square. This gives a neat finish but it is not as strong as the other methods.

BRIDGES

Building bridges was not easy before the development of the arch. A narrow stream could be bridged with a log but a bridge across a wider gap had to be supported from below. Early bridges were built by supporting flat stone slabs on a row of stone pillars or piers set in the riverbed. This only worked if the river was fairly narrow and shallow enough to build the piers. But once the Romans realized that arches could be used to build bridges, wider rivers could be spanned. The Roman built bridges with a series of semicircular arches which cut down on the number of piers needed to support the bridge.

The Chinese were the first to use a shallow arch which could span a wide gap without going too high. The Great Stone Bridge over the River Chiao Shui in China (below) looks very modern even though it was built in A.D. 610. It has a shallow arch with a span of 115 feet (thirty-seven and a half meters). Many modern bridges have a similar shallow arch.

rounded Roman or Norman arch and it also allowed the roof to be vaulted in different ways. The soaring, vaulted roofs of medieval cathedrals were built using stone ribs to support the ceiling above tall, pointed arches. The places where the ribs met on the ceiling were hidden by carvings called "bosses." The tall, graceful arches, large windows and high, delicate ceilings gave these buildings a light and airy appearance which had not been possible before. As stonemasons realized what beautiful effects they could create, the patterns of ribs and bosses grew more and more elaborate and decorative.

Gothic stonemasons needed to find a way to support the weight of the heavy stone roofs of the cathedrals. They came up with "flying buttresses," which are shaped like arches, but are detached from the wall at ground level and curve in to meet it higher up.

From the Egyptian pyramids to the European cathedrals, amazing stone buildings have been designed to last for eternity in celebration of gods and kings. All over the world, examples of the work of early builders still stand today as monuments to their great skill and have influenced architecture ever since.

KEEPING TIME

Day and night were the only time divisions that early man needed, but as civilization developed, people needed to know more precise times in order to organize their lives.

From the earliest times, people's lives were organized by the day and night. The sun came up in the morning, bringing light and warmth. This was the time to get work done, make tools and go hunting. At the end of the day, the sun disappeared and the world became colder and dark. This was the time to curl up somewhere warm and go to sleep.

When people began to organize their lives more efficiently, it was no longer enough to know that night would follow day. They wanted to know how much or how little of the day had passed so that they could organize their working routine and plan official gatherings such as meetings and schooling.

Someone must have noticed that the sun changes its position in the sky as the

△ *The first clocks were simply a stick casting a shadow on the ground.*

▷ *For early people, time was divided into day and night. They got up when it became light, and worked, hunted and ate until it was dark. Then, they found a safe place to sleep until morning.*

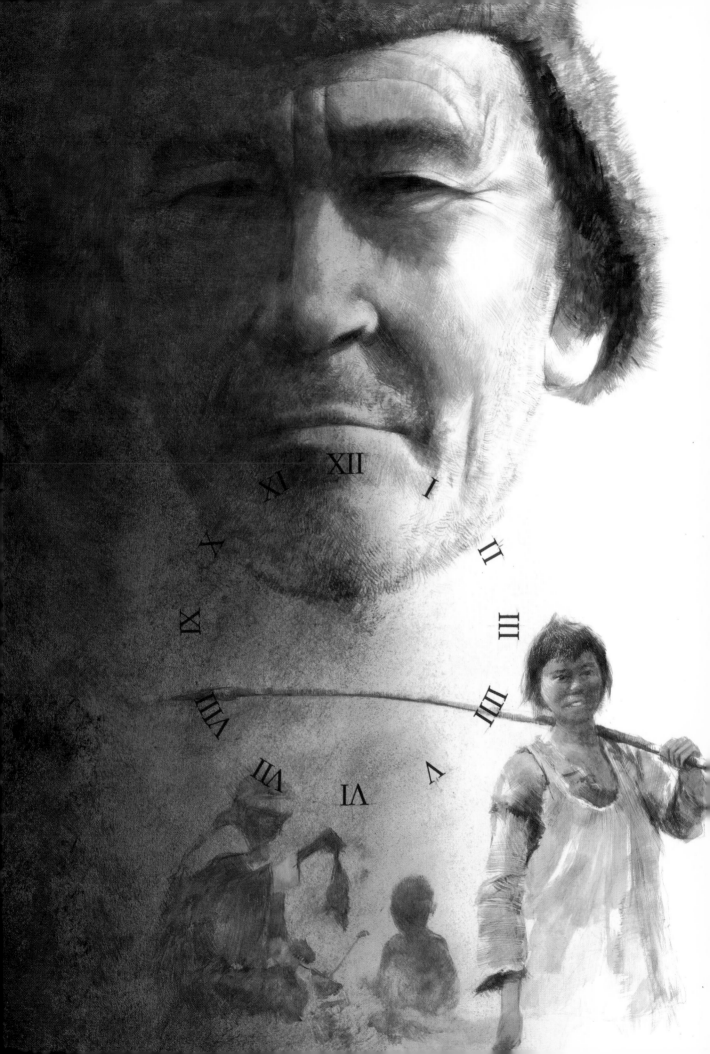

◁ Sundials are often seen high on the walls of old churches. This beautiful angel is from Chartres Cathedral in France and was carved about 1250.

▷ The shadow from the gnomon of a sundial falls at a different angle and is a different length depending on the time of day. It is important that the gnomon points at the Pole Star (in the northern hemisphere). The hour lines also must be aligned with an imaginary band around the Earth's equator.

day progresses, and that a tall straight object such as a pole casts a shadow which moves in a regular pattern each day. The first people to make use of the knowledge were the ancient Egyptians. They realized that the position and length of a shadow on the ground change depending on the height of the sun in the sky at a particular time of day, and that by measuring the shadow, it is possible to tell how much of the day has passed.

The first "clocks" were sticks stuck into the ground. The Egyptians later invented a shadow clock which gave a more accurate indication of time. It was a pole with a crossbar across the top. In the morning, the device was pointed east towards the sun. In the afternoon, it was turned towards the west. The long pole of the clock was divided into twelve equal parts which were marked along its length. The shadow from the crossbar was thrown on to this measuring scale. As the day progressed, the shadow moved further down the measuring scale until nightfall. The length of time we know as an hour came from this Egyptian division of the day into twelve parts between sunrise and sunset.

SUNDIALS

The sundial, which was the main timekeeping device for centuries, usually has a face like a clock with the hours

Sandglasses came in all shapes and sizes. Most timed an hour, but they could be made to measure any length of time.

marked off. A single fixed pointer called a "gnomon" casts a shadow on the dial, and the position of the shadow creeps round the dial as the day passes. Simple sundials were first used in Egypt in about 3500 B.C. In some huge versions, a wall cast a shadow on a flight of steps. Each step represented an hour of the day.

About 300 B.C., a different type of sundial was used in Babylon. It was a solid cube with a half-sphere, or hemisphere, hollowed out of the top. In the center of this hemisphere was a pointer which cast a shadow in the shape of an arc. The arc was divided into twelve equal sections. This sundial was used in the Middle East until the tenth century A.D.

DIVIDING THE DAY

The Greeks used sundials from the third century BC, or perhaps even earlier. Some had flat dials and others used the hemispherical shape of the Babylonian dials. The Tower of Winds in Athens, built in 100 B.C. as an early form of city clock, had eight sundials. The Romans also used sundials from about 290 B.C. The oldest British sundials were the Saxon "scratch dials," which were often carved on a church wall or on a cross in the churchyard. They divided the day into four periods called "tides." The gnomon was fixed to the dial horizontally, and cast its shadow over the marked-out tides.

Sundials were the most accurate timekeepers that people had until the invention of the mechanical clock in the thirteenth century. They became more sophisticated as time went by, and large sundials could tell the correct time to within a minute. Sundials continued to be used for a long time, as mechanical clocks were not always accurate, so sundials made a useful backup for checking on the time.

WATER, WAX AND SAND

Telling the time by the sun has several disadvantages. It is fairly effective in sunny countries like Egypt, Babylon and Greece, but further north the weather is often cloudy so there are no shadows. Also, sundials can not be used for telling the time at night. Early sailors told the time by the position of stars on the

eastern horizon of the sky. The night was divided into twelve "watches," a term which is still used by sailors today.

People also needed to tell the time when they were inside their houses, and neither the sun nor the stars could be used for this. So they turned their minds to inventing clocks which worked in other ways. One of these was the water clock which was used in China, Egypt, Greece and Rome. The simplest type was the "clepsydra" used in ancient Greece. Water ran at a steady rate from one bowl into another bowl that had different levels marked in it. Clepsydras were used in Europe until the Middle Ages.

Another type of water clock consisted of a cylinder containing a stick on a floating base. Water was poured into the cylinder at a steady rate. As the cylinder filled, the stick rose in the water, turning a gearwheel. The gearwheel moved a pointer around a clock face, which was divided into twenty-four hours. The Chinese made even more sophisticated water clocks. One of these had a ten-foot (three-meter) wheel which was turned by buckets of water.

This giant, Chinese water clock was built in A.D. 725 by the monk and mathematician I-Hsing. Each paddle on the wheel (below right) was identical in size. As each one filled up, it moved indicators on by a specific amount via the gearing mechanism (below left). The indicators were on the sphere (top), and acted as a calendar for the sun and the moon, as well as showing the hours and quarter hours.

Another early form of clock was a candle marked off in sections. Each section took one hour to burn down. They were widely used during the Middle Ages because they were easily moved around, unlike a water clock. Candle clocks were used by monks to time medieval religious services.

THE HOURGLASS

The sandglass or hourglass was introduced in the fifteenth century. The early sandglass consisted of two pear-shaped glass bulbs joined to each other by a narrow neck. One of the bulbs was nearly filled with sand, then the glass was sealed and the bulbs were fitted into a frame. The neck between the bulbs was made just wide enough for the sand to run from one bulb to another in an hour. Simple egg-timers work on the same principle.

Sandglasses were used until the nineteenth century for timing the watches on board ship. The end of a watch was announced by ringing a bell. The word "clock" comes from the French word "cloche" or the German word "glocke" for "bell." Bells were also used to announce the time in monasteries and castles before the invention of the mechanical clock. The bells were rung by a person called a "clock-jack," who had a sandglass, water clock, or sundial for telling the time.

MECHANICAL CLOCKS

The earliest mechanical clocks appeared

Christian Huygens, maker of the first pendulum clock.

in Europe in the thirteenth century. They were driven by weights. When the clock was fully wound up, the weight was at the top. It gradually descended, releasing energy to drive the mechanism in the clock. When the weight reached the bottom, the clock needed winding again to store more energy. These early clocks were known as "turret clocks" because they had to be mounted high up on a church tower or tall building so that they did not have to be wound up too often. They were made by blacksmiths, not by clock-makers as in later times. There were smaller versions of turret clocks which people could have in their houses, but they also had to be on a wall.

SPRING ENERGY

Clocks driven by a spring mechanism were invented in the middle of the fifteenth century. They were much smaller and less unwieldy than the turret clock. When a spring-operated clock is wound up, energy is stored in the spring. This energy is slowly released to drive the "movement" of the clock. The movement is a system of gearwheels inside the clock, which turn and push the hands around the dial.

Early clocks only had one hand which showed the hour. An hour was later divided into minutes, and clocks with minute hands began to appear in 1670. The minute hand on a clock is longer than the hour hand and it goes around the clock much faster. The hour hand travels around the clock face once every twelve hours, but the minute hand goes around every hour. The hands are mounted on spindles which are connected to the movement. The gearwheels for each hand have different numbers of teeth, so that they can make the hands move at different speeds.

PENDULUMS

The movement turns the hands of the clock, but it is not the part that makes the clock keep time. If the clock spring released all its energy as soon as the clock was wound up, the gearwheels would turn very fast and the hands would spin around the clock. The energy has to be released in regular small amounts to keep moving at the correct speed. This is done by a part called the "escapement."

The pendulum is a type of escapement. The gears of the clock turn a toothed wheel called the escape wheel. The pendulum is attached to the escape wheel by a device called the "pallet." As the wheel turns, one tooth catches in the pallet at a time, and gives it a slight push as it catches it. The pallet passes the movement to the pendulum to keep it swinging.

The escape wheel is also the counting part of the clock. With each swing of the pendulum, the wheel moves on by one tooth. So if the wheel has sixty teeth, it

will make a complete revolution every sixty swings. The escape wheel is connected to a second hand on the clock. If the pendulum makes one complete swing every second, the second hand will go around the clock face once every sixty seconds. The time it takes for a pendulum to make a complete swing to and fro depends on the length of the pendulum.

The Italian astronomer Galileo (1564–1642) realized that pendulums could be timekeepers in 1582 when he was watching a swinging chandelier in Pisa Cathedral. But it took seventy-four years before another astronomer, the Dutchman Christian Huygens (1629–95), made the first pendulum clock in 1656. From then on, many more clocks were made. The first pendulum clocks were weight-driven and hung on the wall. Then, in 1670, an

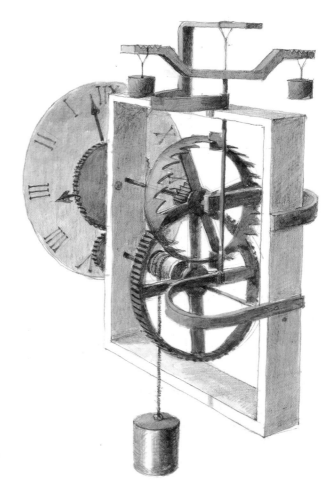

▷ *The earliest mechanical clocks were powered by a weight on a rope which wound around a barrel. As the weight fell, it drove the clock. The escapement is the heavily toothed "crown" wheel above the big wheel driven by the weight. It can be adjusted to go faster or slower by moving the weights (top) on the "foliot". This swings to and fro with each clock beat, and brakes the crown wheel with its "sail" (below).*

THE FIRST WRISTWATCHES

Clocks are fine if you are at home or in a public place where there is one on display. But there are times when people want to know the time and there is no clock in sight. Then, a portable timepiece is needed. The earliest of these was the portable sundial which could be folded flat when it was not being used. Some of these had a direction finder so they doubled as a compass.

Small portable clocks and later pocket-watches developed from the invention of a form of escapement mechanism, the balance wheel. Instead of revolving in one direction, the balance wheel turns first one way and then the other, tightening and releasing a spring.

The first cheap watches were produced in the United States by Robert Ingersoll (1859–1928), who introduced the "dollar watch." It sold in Britain for five shillings (25 pence). Wristwatches were introduced in about 1890 but for many years only women wore them. They became popular with men during the First World War.

English clock-maker named William Clement (born c. 1622) introduced a tall clock with a long pendulum and weights, known as the "grandfather" or "long-case" clock. Many of these early styles of mechanical clocks can still be seen today, alongside their modern electric or battery-operated descendants.

▷ *The "anchor" escapement was perfected by William Clement in the 1670s. As the pendulum swings to the right, the left-hand pallet of the anchor (top) catches the tooth of the escapement wheel, which gives the pallet a push. This makes the pendulum swing to the left, and so on.*

CURES & REMEDIES

Most of the medical practices of long ago seem barbarous or ridiculous today, but some have proved valuable to modern medicine.

Early people knew nothing about the bacteria and viruses that cause disease. A wound caused by a cut or a fall was easy enough to understand, and people could see what had happened if they were ill after eating food that was bad or poisonous. But the sudden onset of a mystery illness was not so easily explained. The only answer early people could find to this problem was that disease must be caused by evil spirits, perhaps because the gods were angry with the people.

MEDICINE MEN

Early cures took the form of rituals to appease the gods or drive out evil spirits. A medicine man or witch doctor would put on an elaborate ceremonial costume and dance to cast out spirits or ask forgiveness of the gods. These methods have nothing to do with medicine as we know it today but they often seemed to work. If the illness was not too serious,

△ *Witch doctors performed rituals intended to drive evil spirits out of the bodies of the sick.*

▷ *Simple medicines were made from plants from the earliest times.*

the person may have recovered naturally and believed it was due to the medicine man. Also, when people had faith in these forms of medicine, they believed they were going to get better, and their positive thinking helped to give them the strength to recover.

Early medicine was not all ritual and magic. Medicine men gradually learned about plants which could be helpful in curing disease. There were also early attempts at surgery. Prehistoric skulls with holes bored in them have been discovered in various parts of the world. This operation, which is called "trepanning," was probably carried out with a pointed flint tool and was intended to allow evil spirits to escape from the brain. The treatment must have been agony, but we know that people survived it because many of the skulls show that the holes in the bone had healed.

SYMPTOMS AND DIAGNOSES

As early civilizations developed, people became more organized in their approach

to medicine. They still believed that everything was controlled by the gods, but there was some training in the administration of plant remedies. Remedies were written down and a record was kept of patients' case histories. Doctors also began to diagnose illnesses by examination and asking the patients questions about their symptoms. In ancient Egypt, doctors were priests who had had medical training. Being a doctor was often a family profession, with fathers passing their medical knowledge to their sons. There were different doctors for different parts of the body. The pharaoh even had a different doctor for each of his eyes!

Egyptian doctors followed many practices carried out by doctors today. They took the patient's pulse and felt their body temperature, though this was simply a matter of feeling whether the person was too hot. They did not know precisely what the pulse or the body temperature should be, but they learned to recognize what was normal. The Egyptians also used splints to mend broken bones and gave patients a wide range of herbal medicines. In Egypt, doctors were paid by the government and

HERBAL REMEDIES

Today, many people have begun to use the herbal cures that were used in the past. Some of the most common herbs have useful properties.

Garlic crushed in oil and rubbed on the chest is good for congestion.

Peppermint tea is good for hiccups.

Sage leaves rubbed on an insect bite will relieve the itching.

Rosemary soaked in oil will help to heal bruises.

▷ *Many herbs have medicinal properties, and herbal remedies have been used for centuries. Today, scientists can extract the useful chemicals in these plants and make them into drugs. For example, the foxglove (center left) contains substances which can be used to treat heart disease. The plant ephedra (center) can be used to make ephedrine to treat low blood pressure and asthma.*

▷ *The four humors were supposed to affect the character as well as health. People governed by air (top left) were supposed to be cheerful; fire (top right) made people hot-tempered; water (bottom left) made them sluggish; and earth (bottom right) made them melancholy.*

△ *Hippocrates, father of modern medicine.*

Galen, the great Roman physician.

patients were treated free if they were traveling or fighting in a war. Although the Egyptians' methods were quite modern in some ways, they still relied on the gods to help out, and their knowledge of the human body was not very great. Cures involved praying to the gods, particularly those with healing properties. People thought that if they made offerings to the priests at the temples of these gods, it would help them to stay in good health.

THE HUMORS

The ancient Greeks were the first people to practice a form of medicine which had nothing to do with religious beliefs. Greek physicians realized that some common symptoms always appear together and that certain medicines brought relief for these symptoms.

The first man to put forward this new theory was Hippocrates (fifth century B.C.,) who lived on the Greek island of Kos. Hippocrates is still said to be the father of medicine. He did not know much about the human body and how it

is made up, but he believed that four elements, fire, air, water and earth, made up the universe and that they had their equivalents in the human body. These were the four "humors," blood, phlegm, yellow bile and black bile. These substances had to be kept balanced in the body. If the balance was disrupted and one of the humors began to dominate the others, a person became ill. The humors theory was incorrect but Hippocrates' methods of diagnosis by careful observation was the basis of medicine for centuries. He was also right about imbalances in the body causing illness and some of his treatments made good sense. For example, if a patient had a raging fever, fire was said to be the element in control of his body, and the balance had to be restored by lowering his temperature.

ROMAN IDEAS

The Romans followed and improved upon many of the ideas put forward by Hippocrates. Galen (c. A.D. 130–200) was a Roman physician, who was born at Pergamum in Asia Minor. He learned that the muscles are controlled by the brain from his work as a doctor to the gladiators' school in Pergamum. Galen later became personal doctor to five of the Roman emperors.

Galen wrote medical works which covered 500 years of study by doctors of Greece and Rome as well as his own findings. He made many mistakes in his own theories because he did not base his arguments on observation of human

ACUPUNCTURE

The Chinese believe that the body contains twelve channels through which the life force chi flows. Each channel is associated with a particular organ of the body. One way to stimulate the flow of chi along the channels is by acupuncture. This involves inserting special needles at certain points along the channels. Acupuncturists use a map of the body with the acupuncture points marked on it. Each point is related to a particular part of the body or to a certain disorder. Acupuncture has been shown to work well for certain ailments and this method of treatment has become popular in the West.

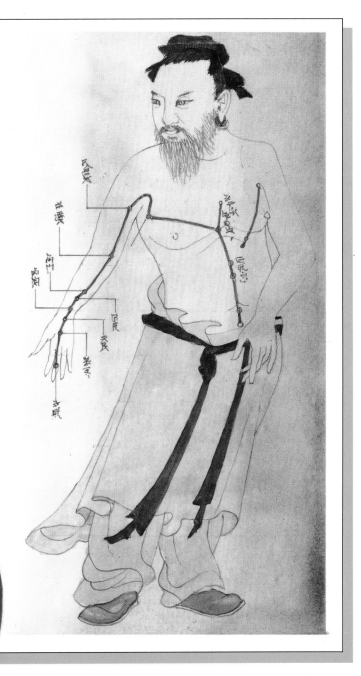

The Chinese symbol of yin and yang.

patients. For example, he thought that the blood passed from one side of the heart to the other but did not realize that it circulated around the body. However, his skill in putting forward his arguments meant that his theories were not challenged for hundreds of years and remained the basis of medical thought for 1,500 years after his death.

IDEAS FROM THE EAST

As with all other aspects of their early civilization, the Chinese developed their medical ideas independently of anyone else. By the sixth century AD, the Chinese had a system of medicine which is still used today. This was the theory of "yin and yang." The Chinese believe that the two opposite forces of yin and yang dominate the world. These forces have to

be balanced for good health. Each organ of the body is either yin or yang, and different circumstances and forces can influence the balance of yin and yang in the body. An imbalance leads to illness.

The Chinese also believe that a life force known as "chi" flows through the body and that this flow must be steady. Many types of Chinese medicine, including acupuncture, are concerned with balancing yin and yang and maintaining a steady flow of chi. Herbs, massage and other forms of natural treatment are used instead of drugs. These forms of medicine are "holistic," that is they aim to treat the whole body rather than just the affected part.

MEDIEVAL MEDICINE

Doctors in the west continued to influence each other but knew nothing of the Chinese approach. After the fall of Rome in the fifth century A.D., there was

△ *Medieval hospitals were run by nuns and monks. Generally, they were considered places to die, as anyone ill enough to go to hospital was unlikely to live.*

no medical teaching in Europe, but the Arabs studied and translated many Greek manuscripts, making useful additions of their own. Rhazes (865–925), chief physician at the hospital in Baghdad, was the first doctor to distinguish between smallpox and measles. The medical works of the Persian writer Avicenna (980–1037) were compulsory reading for European medical students until about 1650.

Medical teaching in Europe was revived in the tenth century, and Latin translations of the medical classics were made from the Arab works. Doctors still followed the teachings of Galen and Avicenna until the sixteenth century when there was a demand for them to start looking for themselves instead of

EARLY OPERATIONS

In the sixteenth century, doctors knew so little about the workings of the human body that internal operations were hardly ever attempted. Amputating or cutting off an infected limb was the most common operation. There were no anesthetics in those days and the patient had to be held down while the limb was sawed off. Many patients either died from the shock of the operation or from infections caused by unhygienic conditions. The stump of the amputated limb was sealed with red-hot iron or boiling pitch to stop the bleeding. The best surgeon of the time was Ambroise Paré (1517–90), a Frenchman who was surgeon general to the armies of three French kings. Paré learned from the wounded soldiers he had to treat and operate on. He introduced new and more effective surgical instruments and a new way of stopping bleeding by tying up the arteries on the stump of an amputated limb. Paré also designed an artificial hand with fingers that moved by springs and small wheels. It was so effective that a soldier could grasp the reins of his horse with the fingers.

slavishly following the words of the ancients. This meant dissecting bodies to find out how they worked.

In 1543, a young Belgian named Andreas Vesalius (1514–64) published the first work on human anatomy based on careful observation of the dissected human body. The work of Vesalius was not really appreciated during his lifetime. People still continued to cling to the theories of Galen. After trying unsuccessfully to promote his teachings, Vesalius gave up and burned all his unpublished manuscripts. But his work was an important step forward. The medical world was ready to move on to finding out for itself, a process that has continued ever since.

▷ *By dissecting bodies, surgeons such as Vesalius and Paré were able to find out more about how the body worked. Unfortunately, many religious people at the time were opposed to the idea of cutting up the bodies of the dead. Vesalius' first dissections were of bodies of criminals that he had stolen from the public gallows.*

Anatomists (people who study the inside of human bodies) were regarded with deep suspicion by most people until well into the nineteenth century.

FURTHER READING

Berger, Gilda. *Religion*. New York: Franklin Watts, 1983.

Caselli, Giovanni. *The First Civilizations*. New York: Peter Bedrick Books, 1983.

Chisholm, Jane and Anne Millard. *Early Civilization*. London: Usborne, 1991.

Conway, Lorraine. *The Middle Ages*. Carthage, IL: Good Apple, 1987.

Endacott, Geoff. *Discovery & Inventions*. New York: Viking, 1991.

Lebrun, Francoise. *The Days of the Cave People*. Lexington, MA: Silver, Burdett & Ginn, 1986.

Macaulay, David. *The Way Things Work*. New York: Dorling Kindersley, 1988.

Macdonald, Fiona. *Everyday Life in the Middle Ages*. Lexington, MA: Silver, Burdett & Ginn, 1985.

———. *Inside a Medieval Cathedral*. New York: Simon & Schuster, 1991.

Makhlouf, Georgia. *The Rise of Major Religions*. Lexington, MA: Silver, Burdett & Ginn, 1988.

McGowen, Tom. *Album of Prehistoric Man*. New York: Macmillan, 1987.

Miquel, Pierre. *Days of Knights & Castles*. Lexington, MA: Silver, Burdett & Ginn, 1985.

Morley, Jacqueline. *Inside an Egyptian Pyramid*. New York: Simon & Schuster, 1991.

Parker, Steve. *The Random House Book of How Things Work*. New York: Random House, 1991.

Reid, Struan. *Usborne Illustrated Handbook of Invention and Discovery*. London: Usborne, 1986.

Stidworthy, John. *When Humans Began*. Lexington, MA: Silver, Burdett & Ginn, 1986.

Turvey, Peter. *Inventions: Inventors & Ingenious Ideas*. New York: Franklin Watts, 1992.

Wood, Tim. *Prehistoric People*. New York: Franklin Watts, 1980.

INDEX

Acupuncture, 87, 88
"Adobe," 59
Adz, 21
Air ("humor"), 84, 86
"Alloy," first, 21
Amputations, 89
Anatomists, 89
"Anchor" escapement, 81
Animal magic, 32
Animals
    domestication of,
        38–39, 40
    pulling plows, 44,
        46, 47
    types farmed, 41
"Annealing," 49
Arches
    construction, 68–70
    Mayan, 63
    pointed, 70, 72–73
Architecture
    early, 54
    orders of columns, 67.
    See also Stone, building
        with
"Ard," 45, 48
Arteries, tying, 89
Auger, 22
Avicenna, 88
Awl, 19
Aztec civilization,
    buildings, 64

Babylonian sundial, 77
Barrel vaults, 70
"Bartering," 41
Beehive houses, 54
Bells, time-keeping by, 79
Black bile ("humor"), 84
Blood ("humor"), 86
Body painting, 30
Bone tools, 11, 19, 20
Bones
    as building material, 54,
        55
    use in rituals, 32
"Bosses," 73
Bow drill, 19
    making fire with, 24, 29
Brace and bit, 22
Bread making, 38–39
Brick
    as facing material, 70.
    See also Mud bricks
Bridges, early
    construction, 73
Bronze tools, 21
    clamps, 66

Burials, first, 30
    gifts for the dead,
        32–34
Buttresses, 71
    function, 72
Byzantine domes, 72

Candle clocks, 79
Carpenters, 21
    medieval, 22
    Roman, 22
"Cast iron," 48–49
Catal Hüyük, Turkey,
    41, 54
Cathedrals, Gothic, 71,
    73
Caves, as shelter, 52
"Chi," 87, 88
China, ancient
    bridge construction,
        73
    fire, use of , 24
    medicine, 87–88
    plow development,
        47–50
    time-keeping, 78
    tools, 15
Chisels, metal, 21
Choukoutien cave,
    China, 15, 24
Clement, William, 81
"Clepsydra," 78
"Clock-jack," 79
Clocks
    first, 74, 75
    hands, 79–80
    mechanical, 78, 79
        power for, 80
    spring-driven, 79–80
Clothes and costumes
    ceremonial, 30
        medicine men, 82
    making, 19, 20, 21
"Coffering," 68, 72
Coins, 41
Colosseum, Rome, 68
Concrete
    building with, 68
        vaults of, 70, 72
    Roman, 66–67, 68
Cooking, development
    of, 26–27, 29
Copper tools, 21, 62
"Corbeling," 68, 72
"Core tool," 13, 14
Corinthian columns, 67
Craft-workers
    and trade, 40
    need for raw
        materials, 41
Crops

first, 38
    harvesting, 40
    types grown, 41
    watering, 42
Cures, 82–89
Curves, building in,
    67–68
Cuzco, Peru, 64

Death. **See** Life and
    death
Diagnoses, medical,
    84–86
Dissection, medical need
    for, 89
"Dollar watch," 81
Domed roofs, 68
    on a square building,
        72
    supporting, 70–72
Doric columns, 67
Draft beam, 49
Drills, early, 19

Earth ("humor"), 84, 86
East India Companies,
    50
Egypt, ancient
    doctors, 84–86
        cures and remedies,
            84, 86
        gods, 34
        plows, 45–46, 48
        pyramids, 61–62
        time-keeping, 77
Ephedra, medicinal
    properties, 84
Ephedrine (drug), 84
Escape wheel, 80
"Escapement," 80, 81
Evil spirits, driving out,
    82

"Facing," brick, 70
Farming
    earliest tools, 20, 21
    effect of the plow, 51
    implements. **See** Plow;
        Sickle
    religious beliefs and,
        34–35
    spread of, 42
    where did it start?,
        39–40.
    See also Crops
Fevers, early remedy
    for, 86
Fire
    and human evolution,
        29
    as a "humor," 84, 86

as protection, 26, 27
    making, 24–29
        early techniques,
            27–29
"Fire lenses," 27
Fireplaces and hearths,
    early, 29
Fish gods, 32
Fishing, development of,
    38
"Flake tools," 13, 14, 19
Flint
    for fire making, 29
    mining for, 21
    tools, 11, 12–21
Flying buttresses, 71, 73
Food
    growing, 36–43.
    See also Farming
    new sources of, 38–39
    as religious offering,
        32, 34
Foxglove, medicinal
    properties, 84

Galen, 86, 88
    mistakes in theories,
        86–87
Galileo, 80
Garlic remedy, 84
"Gnomon," 76, 77
"Goat-song," 32
Goats
    domestication of, 36
    religious importance,
        32
Gods
    early, 34–35
    and illness, 84, 86
Gothic architecture, 71,
    72–73
    vaults, 70
"Grandfather" clock, 81
Granite, building with,
    62
Grasses, domestication
    of, 40
Graves, first, 30–32
Great Pyramid, Giza, 62
Great Stone Bridge,
    China, 73
Greece, ancient
    building methods,
        64, 66
    column decoration, 67
    medicine, 86
    religious belief, 32, 35
    time-keeping, 77, 78

"Hafting," 20
Hagia Sophia,

Constantinople, 72
Hal Saflieni temples, Malta, 61
Hand, artificial, 89
Hand-axes
  flint, 12, 14–15, 16
  metal, 21, 22
"Handy man," 12
Harappa (city), India, 54
Hearths. **See** Fireplaces and hearths
Herbal remedies, 84
Herbs, medicinal properties, 84
Hippocrates, 86
"Holistic" medicine, 88
"Hominids," 12
Homo erectus, 12, 14–15, 16
  speech, 27
  use of fire, 24–27
Homo habilis, 12
Homo sapiens, 12
Homo sapiens neanderthalis, 12, 32
Homo sapiens sapiens, 12, 19–20
  clothes, 21
Hospitals, medieval, 88
Hour-glasses. **See** Sand-glasses
Houses, changing shapes of, 59. **See also** Huts
Human beings, evolution of, 11–12
Humors, 84, 86
Hunter-gatherers, 42
Huts
  made from branches, 54, 55, 57
  wooden, 58
Huygens, Christian, 79, 80
  pendulum clocks, 81
"Hüyük," 40

Igloos, 56
Inca civilization, buildings, 64
Ingersoll, Robert, 81
Intersecting vault, 70
Inuit shelters, 56
Ionic columns, 67
Iron
  clamps, 66
  plowshares, 48
  tools, 21
Iron pyrites, 29
Ironworking,

development of, 49–50
Irrigation systems, 42

Jefferson, Thomas, 50, 51
Jericho, Palestine, 41, 54

"Keystone," 70

Lamps, early, 29
Lathe, wood-turning, 22
Leakey, Louis, 16
Lepenski Vir settlement, Serbia, 32, 58
Life and death, 30–35
Limestone, building with, 66
"Long-case" clock, 81
"Lost city," 64

Machu Picchu, Peru, 64
Marble, building with, 66
Markets, development of, 41
Massage, 88
Mayan civilization, buildings, 63
Medical teaching, revival of, 88–89
Medicine (practice of)
  cures and remedies, 82–89
  ideas from the East, 87–88
  medieval, 88–89
Medicine men, 82–84
Medicines
  from plants, 82. **See also** Herbal remedies
"Megaliths," 61
Mesopotamia
  development of farming, 45–46, 48
  houses, 54
Mirrors, obsidian, 41
Mohenjo-daro, India, 54
"Mortise and tenon" joints, 64
"Moldboard," 50–51
"Movement" (clock), 79
Mud bricks
  making, 59
  huts and houses of, 55, 56, 58–59, 64
Music and dance
  earliest instruments, 33–34

ritualistic, 30, 33–34
Mycenaean buildings, 68
Neanderthal burials, 32
Needles, bone, 20

"Obsidian," 41
Olduvai Gorge, Tanzania, 16
Open field system, 51
Operations, 89
  earliest, 84
Oxen, use on farms, 44, 46, 47

"Pallet," 80
Pan P'o Ts'un houses, China, 58
Pantheon, Rome, 68, 70, 72
Paré, Ambroise, 89
Parthenon, Athens, 64
Pebble tools, 12–14
Pendulums, 80–81
Peppermint remedy, 84
Phlegm ("humor"), 86
Plane, carpenter's, 22
Plows and plowing, 44–51, 48–49
  pulling the plow, 44, 46, 47, 48
Plowshares, development of, 47–48
Pocket-watches, 81
Pons Fabricius, Rome, 70
Pyramids, construction methods, 61–62, 63, 64

"Querns," 38

Rafters, 56
Refuge. **See** Shelter
Religious ceremonies
  earliest, 30, 33, 35
Remedies. **See** Cures
Rhazes, 88
Ribbed vaults, 70
"Ribs," 70, 72, 73
Ridge poles, 58
Rituals
  early, 30
  Native American, 33
Roman Empire
  bridge construction, 73
  building methods, 66–67
  use of the arch, 68–70
  medicine, 86–87

plow, 48
tools, 22
Ropes
  animal sinew, 57
  powering a clock with, 80
Rosemary remedy, 84

Sage remedy, 84
Sand-glasses, 77, 79
Saws
  flint, 19
  metal, 21, 22
  Roman, 22
"Scratch dials," 77
Scratch plows, 45–46
Seed sowing, early, 44–45
Shadow clock, 77
"Shaduf," 42
Shanidar cave, Iraq, 33
Sharmans, 33
Shelter, 52–59
Sickles, 40
  development of, 20, 21
"Slash and burn agriculture," 36
"Squinch arches," 72
Steam engines, use in farming, 48
Stilts, houses on, 56
"Stock," 50
Stone
  building with, 54, 60–73
  carved and painted, 67
  plowshares of, 47–48
  quarrying, 60, 61
  transporting
    for pyramids, 61–62
    for Stonehenge, 60. **See also** Flint; Pebble tools
Stone-working techniques, 15
Stonehenge, England, 30, 60, 64
Strip farming, 51
Sumerians
  religious beliefs, 35
  trading, 41
Sundials, 76, 77
  portable, 81
Surgical instruments, 89
  ancient, 84
Symptoms, 84–86
  medicines for, 86

Tarxien temples, Malta, 61

"Tell," 40
Temples
    Aztec, 64
    Greek and Roman, 64,
        66–67
    Maltese, 61
    Mayan, 63
Tenochtitlán, Mexico,
    64
Tents, skin, 52, 55, 56,
    57–58
Terra Amata settlement,
    France, 54
Teshik-Tash grave,
    Uzbekistan, 32
Thatched roofs, 56, 58
"Tholoi," 54
"Tides," 77
Time-keeping, 74–81
    at sea, 78
"Tool-making man," 12
Tools/toolmaking
    for boring, 19
    buried with dead, 32
    for farming, 20–21
    first, 11–23
    of hominids, 12–14
    implements for
        making, 20
    Inca, 64
    "Levalloisian"
        method, 15–16
    metal, 19
    Neanderthal, 16–19
    obsidian, 41
    for pyramid building,
        62
    for working wood,
        21–22.
    See also Surgical
        instruments
"Totems," 35
Tower of the Winds,
    Athens, 77
Town walls, 54
Towns
    early layout, 54
    first, 40–41
    grid layout, 54
    trade links, 41
Tractors, pulling plows
    with, 48, 51
Trading
    earliest, 40
    without money, 41
    and the plow, 50–51
    value of goods, 41
Treasury of Atreus, 68
"Trepanning," 84
"Turret clocks," 79

Vault construction,
    70–71
Vesalius, 89
Vice, carpenter's, 22
Vilcabamba, Peru, 64

Walls, concrete, 68
"Watches," 78
Water ("humor"), 84, 86
Water clocks, 78
Wattle and daub huts,
    55, 58, 64
Weapons
    hardening with fire, 27
"Wise man," 16
Witch doctors, 82
Wood
    building with, 52–54
    plows of, 46–47,
        48–49
    tools of, 11, 20
    working in
        tools for, 21–22
Wristwatches, 81
"Wrought iron," 48

Yellow bile ("humor"),
    86
"Yin and yang," 87–88